TOGETHER
Five Enduring Principles for Effective Teamwork

by

BRUCE HILLS

CHI–Books
PO Box 6462
Upper Mt Gravatt, Brisbane
QLD 4122
Australia

www.chibooks.org
publisher@chibooks.org

Together: *Five Enduring Principles for Effective Teamwork*
Copyright © 2020 by Bruce Hills

Print ISBN: 978-0-6485108-1-9
eBook ISBN: 978-0-6485108-2-6

Under International Copyright Law, all rights reserved. No part of this eBook may be reproduced, stored in a retrieval system, or transmitted in any form, including by any means electronic, mechanical, photocopying or otherwise in whole or in part without permission in writing from the publisher, except in the case of sermon preparation, reviews or articles and brief quotations embodied in critical articles. The use of occasional page copying for personal or group study is permitted and encouraged. Permission will be granted upon request.

Unless otherwise indicated, all Scripture quotations are taken from the *Holy Bible*, New Living Translation, Copyright © 1996, 2004. Used by permission of Tyndale House Publishers, Inc., Carol Stream, Illinois 60188. All rights reserved.

Printed in Australia, United Kingdom and the United States of America.

Distributed in the USA and Internationally by Ingram Book Group and Amazon. Also available from others like: Bookdepository.co.uk and Koorong.com (Australia).

Distribution of eBook version: Amazon Kindle, Apple iBooks, Koorong.com and others like Barnes & Noble NOOK and KOBO.

Editorial assistance: Anne Hamilton

Cover design: Dave Stone

Layout: Jonathan Gould

TOGETHER

Five Enduring Principles for Effective Teamwork

by

BRUCE HILLS

DEDICATION

To the leaders of World Outreach International — the most gifted, dedicated and geographically diverse team I have had the honour of leading. This book is dedicated to you.

By the same author

INSIDE OUT
A Biblical and Practical Guide to Self-leadership

FEARPROOF
How to Overcome the Paralyzing Power of Fear – Exploring the 'do not fear' statements of the Old Testament

PRAYING WITH POWER
How to Engage in a Deeper Level of Personal Prayer by Praying the Scriptures

You can purchase other titles by Bruce Hills from:
www.amazon.com
www.koorong.com.au
www.bookdepository.co.uk

eBooks also available from Amazon Kindle; Apple iBookstore; Koorong.com and others like Barnes & Noble NOOK and KOBO

CONTENTS

Foreword by Mark Varughese 1

Introduction 3

SECTION I – TANGIBLE LOVE 9
    Chapter 1   TANGIBLE LOVE 11
                    Who we are to love 13
                    How teams are to love one another 15
                    Why we are to love 23

SECTION II – SELFLESS UNITY 27
    Chapter 2   SELFLESS UNITY (Part One) 29
                    Working together 30
                    Resolve conflicts quickly and biblically 36
                    Be others-centred 44
    Chapter 3   SELFLESS UNITY (Part Two) 53
                    Adopt the attitude of a servant leader 53
                    Pray for and with each other 58
                    Support the team leader and his/her vision 61

SECTION III – CLEAR COMMUNICATION 69
    Chapter 4   CLEAR COMMUNICATION (Part One) 71
                    Speak the truth in love 71
                    Utilise good communication channels 79
                    Develop listening skills 83
    Chapter 5   CLEAR COMMUNICATION (Part Two) 89
                    Encourage one another 89
                    Speak well of each other and to each other 94
                    Clarify tasks and responsibilities 97

SECTION IV – AUTHENTIC RELATIONSHIP 101
    Chapter 6   AUTHENTIC RELATIONSHIP (Part One) 103
                      Be real with one another 103
                      Be committed to one another 104
                      Proactively get to know each other 107
    Chapter 7   AUTHENTIC RELATIONSHIP (Part Two) 111
                      Develop trust in one another 111
                      Display loyalty to one another 120
                      Keep a forgiving spirit 126

SECTION V – RESPECTFUL HONOUR 133
    Chapter 8   RESPECTFUL HONOUR 135
                      Honour God 137
                      Honour our leaders 140
                      Honour one another 144

Conclusion 149

Appendix .... Five Spheres of Christian Leadership 153

Bibliography 157

FOREWORD

My wife and I have had the privilege of knowing Bruce Hills for many years. Beyond our friendship is our deep admiration and gratitude for his godly example, his love for people, his strategic mind and his vast experience which has impacted so many around the world.

Having led a very significant church, worked extensively on the mission field with teams and currently leading a global missional organisation (amongst many other experiences in serving God so faithfully over decades) means that the powerful and practical wisdom in this book is a refined work that has been personally tested in a myriad of settings and seasons.

Psalm 133 highlights the benefits of teams who are united – a 'good and pleasant' experience, a commanded blessing, 'life' forevermore, as well as the accelerated impact on those who are working together.

Every leader and team member want to be part of a united, healthy authentic environment which awakens purpose, multiplies productivity and brings great outcomes to all involved. The challenge is never the theory – it's always in the application.

Kingdomcity (*the church I lead*) has expanded into multiple countries with diversity in ethnicity, socio-economic status, language, mindset and culture in general. As a result, much of my time is spent attempting to create a healthy, united 'kingdom' culture within our global leadership and their teams in spite of the diversity.

Underlying this task is the clear conviction that although there will be variances in application because of cultural diversity, the 'kingdom' principles that govern our culture are foremost, not just because our devotion to Christ should supersede our personal culture, but because God's ways and His values are always better and are applicable in every culture.

There's no shortage of material highlighting the power of vision, the importance of values and most competent leaders can articulate this well, but teams often come undone because they don't know the 'how' – i.e. *how do we do create these values, what does that look like, can you break that down for me please…?*

This is the brilliance of *'Together: Five Enduring Principles for Effective Teamwork'.*

All 5 keys – **Tangible Love, Selfless Unity, Clear Communication, Authentic Relationship and Respectful Honour** are introduced biblically and then expounded practically. What each value *looks* like, *how* to create these ideals, practical examples, the dangers of the absence of these values, as well as vulnerable and personal stories from Bruce's life and experience makes this so beneficial for every team member and leader.

I wholeheartedly agree with all 5 values and thoroughly enjoyed reading this. I'm delighted to not only recommend that you read this, but also practically apply it personally and with your teams using the engaging discussion questions at the end of each chapter. The wisdom in these pages will enhance every person who reads it and applies it.

Mark Varughese
Global Pastor
Kingdomcity Church, Perth, Australia

INTRODUCTION

Some years ago, I taught my five-year-old granddaughter how to ride her newly acquired bike on the basketball court of a nearby school. On the way home, I was pushing her bike up a grassy hill in our local park. She came alongside the bike, took hold of the other handle bar, so that we were now both pushing the bike uphill. She looked at me and said, 'Bampy (Welsh for grandpa), this is teamwork.' I was amazed that someone so young even understood the concept of teamwork, let alone knew the word. She was perfectly right–it was teamwork.

Teamwork is an immensely efficient way to get a job done. Effective teamwork has many components such as a defined purpose, stated objectives, a competent leader, clear communication, efficient organisation and a sense of comradery.

One of the most underrated, but indispensable, qualities of a productive team is relationship, where the team is not just linked by a common purpose, but meshed together by authentic relationships.

In a Christian leadership context, one of the primary purposes of team is not just task, but relationship. Task is secondary; relationships are primary. If relationship is the root, task is the fruit. If relationship is not the root, task will not reach its potential. I am convinced that for a task to truly be accomplished in a way that honours the Lord and bears godly fruit, it must be done out of relationship. If team relationships are superficial, the purpose of the team will be hampered and constricted.

This book will centre on the relational aspect of a team because it is one of the most vital to get the job done. To do so, I will articulate five relational principles for an effective and productive team. Before doing so, there's a very important foundational question.

Why are relationships on the team so imperative?

There are practical, theological and Scriptural answers to this vital question.

A first answer to the question of why team relationships are crucial is a *practical* one. A team working together in relationship is vital because it is the most effectual way to accomplish a task. As Ecclesiastes 4:9-12 says, *'Two are better off than one, for they can help each other succeed…Three are even better, for a triple-braided cord is not easily broken.'* Put simply, more can be accomplished by a team of people working with one heart and one mind toward a common purpose than by individuals doing their own thing, no matter how competent they may be. This is the principle of synergy that we'll have a look at in Chapter Two. According to Paul, in his metaphor of the many-membered body of Christ, we see that only when each part does its work in harmony with the other members does the body rise to its full potential in purpose and maturity. It's the same with teams.

Secondly, there is a *theological* reason why relationships on a team are essential. A team joined together in relationship to fulfil a godly purpose reflects God in his essential nature and work as Trinity. The inter-relationship and interdependence of Father, Son and Holy Spirit, as Trinity,[1] is the pre-eminent model of team and teamwork. The three divine Persons are so closely bound together in love that they're indivisibly one.

Through God's great works of Creation (Genesis 1:1) and Redemption (Matthew 3:16-17; John 14:6, 16-17, 17:21-23), we see a revelation of the three Persons working together in divine purpose. From this revelation, we find grounding for the patterns and principles of team such as: love (1 John 4:16; John 15:9; 17:23-26), interdependence (Acts 10:38; John 4:34, 5:19, 6:38, 9:4, 14:24), unity (John 17:20-23) and submission (John 14:28; Philippians 2:6-8). Therefore, a team of redeemed persons-in-relationship echoes God as a tri-unity of divine persons-in-relationship.

Then, thirdly, there is a *Scriptural* reason why relationships on a team are so necessary. Teams are a Biblical pattern. Some examples of teams in the Bible are Moses and Aaron (Exodus 4:16), Caleb and Joshua (Numbers 14:6), Elijah and Elisha (2 Kings 2:6), the seventy sent out two by two (Luke 10:1), and, of course, Jesus and the twelve apostles. After Pentecost, there were numerous teams of people, principally apostles, who ministered in teams.[2] A study of Paul's ministry in Acts and his writing in the Epistles reveals that at least 36 people (out of the 100 or so mentioned being associated with him) were, at some point and to some degree, part of his ministry team(s).[3] Paul never worked alone. From the very outset of his apostolic ministry, he was involved in teams. In short, teams are seen all through God's Word as a way by which God's purposes are carried out.

If relationships on a team are essential because, firstly, the practical reason that two (or more) are better than one to get a job done, secondly, theologically, a team working in unity for a godly purpose echoes God in his essence and actions as Trinity, and, thirdly, teams are a Scriptural way to accomplish a God-given purpose, then how does a team work together relationally? I will now propose five principles as a way of doing so.

Brief summary of the five relational principles of a team

This book is divided into five sections that will address each of the five relational principles. Each section contains a chapter or chapters that will explain, illustrate and apply each one. In short, the five principles are:

1. Tangible Love – teams needed to be marked and motivated by love
2. Selfless Unity – teams need to be of one heart and mind working together for a common purpose
3. Clear Communication – teams need to communicate efficiently and effectively
4. Authentic Relationships – teams need to be characterised by genuine relationships
5. Respectful Honour – teams need to express inward and outward honour to one another

Perspective

Everything I have written about has been tried and tested from my own or other's personal experiences. I have been on many teams, led teams, established teams, taken over teams, grown teams, and was once rejected by a team. I have been part of highly successful teams and participated in highly dysfunctional teams. On various teams, I have experienced successes and failures, periods of joy and misery, along with times of incredible productivity and times of frustrating unfruitfulness. In relational terms, I have been on teams with great chemistry and comradery, but on others with division and disharmony.

A very important point, too, is that, in my present role, I am a team leader. What I've written in this book is not theoretical, but the principles the team I lead endeavour to live by.

Though the principles I'll articulate are applicable in many settings, this book is framed within the context of a Christian leadership team; that is, a team serving in a local church or Christian ministry/organization.

I've purposefully used inclusive pronouns, such as 'we' and 'our', wherever possible, so that we're journeying together. However, at times, I will propose some practical suggestions, so the pronouns will shift to 'you' and 'your'.

Another perspective to keep in mind is *cultural*. I was born, raised and educated in Australia. My theological, Biblical and ministry training was in Australian colleges. All my pastoral experience has been in Australian churches. However, I have had extensive ministry experience in cross-cultural mission, both home and abroad. I am certainly no expert, but mixing with people of other cultures in many contexts has opened my eyes to cultural nuances and interpretations. At first reading, some things I write may not be palatable or pertinent in your culture, but I encourage you to identify the principles I'm seeking to convey and wrestle with how they're applicable in your cultural setting.

Personal and team reflection
At the end of every major point and chapter I have added some questions for your personal reflection and discussion with your team. The purpose of including these questions is for you and your team to honestly and transparently assess yourself and your team. If, as I'm hoping, the reflection is helpful, you'll be able to individually and collectively formulate actions or changes to make the team more relational.

Please don't just gloss over the questions, but interact with them, especially as a team. In this way, you're more likely to maximise the impact for you personally and the team.

Let's begin…

SECTION I

Tangible Love

CHAPTER 1
Tangible Love

Emperor penguins can teach us a lot about teamwork. Spending their entire lives in Antarctica, Emperor penguins are the only penguin species that breeds during winter. From the sea's edge, they trek along ice for 50-120 kilometres to breeding colonies where the female lays a single egg, before returning to the ocean to feed. Her male breeding partner then incubates the egg over two months, withstanding some of the coldest, windiest and harshest conditions on earth.[4]

The males endure the coldest environment of any bird by forming very tight and compact huddles (also known as the turtle formation), ranging in number from ten to hundreds. As they do so, each penguin leans forward onto a neighbour. Then they slowly shuffle to the side in a collective spiral which gives each penguin a turn on the outside and the inside. This instinctive action means that no penguin endures the conditions alone, but shares it equally. The tightness of their bond traps heat inside the huddle, ensuring warmth for themselves, their fellow penguins, and, most importantly, the eggs and recently hatched chicks (nestlings).[5]

The Emperor penguins' close bonds are a remarkable example from the natural world of the relationships that should characterise teams. It is a vivid picture of the first relational principle of team we'll explore, which is *love*.

Love is the foremost principle of team ministry. Love should undergird the whole fabric and function of a team. Without love, everything a team does is superficial and cosmetic. Without love, a team defaults to duty or task. Without love, a team can quickly dissolve into factions and silos.

There are many exhortations in the New Testament for Christians to love another (Romans 13:8; 1 Thessalonians 4:9; 1 Peter 1:22). Loving one another was a particular theme of the apostle John's writings (1 John 3:11, 4:7, 4:11-12; 2 John 5). I want to focus on the one reference to 'loving one another' that was spoken to a team. Found in John 13:34-35, it records the words of Jesus speaking to his disciples (cf. John 15:12,17). This chapter will examine these words of Jesus and their application to contemporary teams.

New Command

In John 13, the public ministry of Jesus was over. Nothing more would be spoken to the crowds. Jesus had gathered with his team for one last meal. While they were eating, Judas, under satanic inspiration, prepared to betray Jesus (John 13:2, 27). Meanwhile, Jesus, under divine inspiration, prepared his disciples for their ministry once he had completed his mission. After washing the disciples' feet (13:3-17), Jesus predicted his betrayal (13:18-29). No sooner had he done so than Judas left the room, literally and figuratively from the light into the night (13:30). The disciples were ignorant of Judas' sinister and subversive mission of treachery (13:29).

> **Love should undergird the whole fabric and function of a team.**

After Judas left, Jesus began to speak about how the time had come for him to fulfil his redemptive mission. Every conceivable emotion must have filled his heart as Jesus simultaneously felt the betrayal of a close friend *and* the glory of fulfilling his redemptive mission that would bring honour to his Father (13:21, 31-32).

Jesus' next words were very poignant and pertinent. These words not only had immense significance for his disciples at the time, but have compelling significance for teams today:

> *'A new command I give you: Love one another. As I have loved you, so you must love one another. By this all men will know that you are my disciples, if you love one another.'* (John 13:34-35)

From these three sentences, we'll now explore *who* we are to love, *how* we are to love them and *why* we need to love the other people on a team.

1. WHO WE ARE TO LOVE

I was intrigued by Jesus' use of the word *'new'* command (John 13:34). The command to love others was not a new command (cf. 1 John 2:7-8), but a very old one, dating back to Old Testament Law. In Leviticus 19:18, the Israelites were required to *'love your neighbour as yourself'*. So, what was actually *new* about the command? The answer to that question is partially that the *object* of their love was new. Jesus modified the word *'neighbour'* to the words *'one another'*. He was commanding and challenging his disciples to love *each other*. Love was to be the distinguishing feature of the team. Jesus defined *who* they were to love.

As we seek to comprehend the implications of Jesus' command, let's consider the relational climate among the disciples. Jesus' team of disciples was an eclectic group in terms of their ages, temperaments and backgrounds. Their diversity brought complexity and tension to their relationships. Up to this point, we read in the Gospels of the disciples' selfish interests, unhealthy ambition (Mark 10:35-37), friction (Mark 10:41) and a festering debate about who was the most important (Luke

22:24). Yet into this mix of dispositions and emotions Jesus issued the command for them to love each other.

What does this mean for us and our teams? In the same way that Jesus prayerfully selected twelve men to be on his team, we have been chosen to be on the teams in which we serve. As the twelve were joined together by God, so God has joined us with the other members of our teams. As there were obvious diversities and differences between the disciples, so there are sure to be on our teams. The implied question in all this is whether we truly love each other? It's relatively easy to love those who love us or love those who are like us. Jesus' command overrides our own prejudices and preferences and urges us to love *all* those with whom we are joined on our team.

We need to do some self-reflection by asking some personal, evaluating questions to determine the level of love we bring to the team.

- Am I interested and engaged with the other team members, or am I superficial, disinterested or disengaged?
- Do I have a genuine concern for the welfare of the other team members, or am I just concerned about my own wellbeing and personal interests?
- Do I treat them as I want to be treated or do I treat them as affected by my mood, emotions or prejudice?
- Am I working to dismantle barriers, change attitudes and foster relationships, or am I leaving obstacles and attitudes unaddressed by keeping to myself?
- Do I actively pray for my team members or do I just pray about my own needs?

Let me spell it out: according to Jesus, if we are part of a team, we are called not only to work with them, but to authentically *love* them.

2. HOW TEAMS ARE TO LOVE ONE ANOTHER

Now that we know *who* we are to love, a second major question is *how* are we to demonstrate our love to our fellow team members?

Jesus gave us a model for how we are to express love to the other members of our team. In the second sentence of John 13:34, Jesus said, 'As I have loved you, *so you must love one another'* (emphasis mine). Put simply, the love the disciples were to demonstrate to each other must be modelled on the way that Jesus had loved them. Jesus embodied and exemplified the nature of the love he wanted his disciples to express to one another. The love he spoke of was not just an emotion or feeling, but actions that flowed from the core of our being.

After setting the context, John 13:1 (NIV) records that, *'having loved his own who were in the world, he now showed them the* full extent *of his love'* (emphasis mine). As defined by Jesus' example, what does it mean for us to love one another to the full extent?

Love, based on the model of Jesus' love, is IDENTIFICATION with one another

A first demonstration of how Jesus loves us is that he *identified* with us. Jesus did so through the incarnation, when he (the Word) became flesh (John 1:14). He was fully God, but he came as fully man. In so doing, he became one of us. His coming was the initiative of God, who *'so loved the world that he gave his one and only Son'* (John 3:16). Through Jesus, the Lord reached out to us and met us at the point of our human predicament caused by sin. We could do nothing. We were powerless. Jesus' coming as our Lord and Saviour was all *God's* initiative, motivated by his love and grace.

What we learn from Jesus' example is that love initiates and identifies with others at the point of their need. If we are to love

> **We must not wait for people to come to us; we must go to them. We meet them at the point of their need.**

one another 'as he loved us' we, too, must identify with people. We must initiate contact, rather than wait for them to come to us. We must show an interest in them rather than wait for them to show an interest in us. We must change rather than wait for them to change. We must not wait for people to come to us; we must go to them. We meet them at the point of *their* need.

By way of illustration, some years ago I heard an American preacher share the following story at a conference. He was pastoring a relatively large church of several thousand people in Louisiana. To make the church personal and relational, they had hundreds of small groups that met during the week for fellowship, prayer and Bible Study. One such group was comprised of a group of ladies, who loved and cared for each other.

After some time, one of the ladies was diagnosed with leukemia. Her name wasn't revealed, but for the sake of the story, I'll call her Jennifer. When Jennifer began her treatment, one of the side effects was hair loss. Initially, it was just a few strands of hair, which she skilfully covered over with scarves and head bands. In time, though, large clumps began to fall out, exposing Jennifer's scalp which became difficult to disguise. When bald patches became visible and prominent, she was very embarrassed and stopped attending her church's public worship services. Then, when almost all her hair had fallen out, she slowly began to withdraw from her small group, eventually becoming a virtual hermit in her home. Jennifer, understandably, didn't want to be seen without hair.

Her friends were saddened by her self-imposed isolation and decided on a plan to reach out to her. One of them rang her and, on behalf of the group, told her that all the ladies were coming to her home the following week to have their small group. Instead of Jennifer having to go out in public, the group were going to come to her in private. She tried to dissuade them, but they were insistent. Despite her polite protestations, they were lovingly determined to come to her the following week.

True to their arrangement, all the ladies arrived at Jennifer's home in unison the following week. One of them knocked on the door. Jennifer reluctantly and tentatively opened the door. As she did so, she was astonished and flabbergasted by what she saw. All of her friends had shaved their hair off and stood on Jennifer's landing with bald heads. Instead of Jennifer having to feel embarrassed or isolated by her predicament, her friends *identified* with her by becoming like her. We can only imagine the emotional scenes that transpired at Jennifer's home that day.

In the same way that Jennifer's friends identified with her, if we are to love the other people on our team based on the way Jesus loved his disciples, then our love must be incarnational; that is, it should be embodied, visible, tangible and demonstrable. Phrased differently, if we are to identify with one another, we do so by initiating actions of love in word and deed.

Love, based on the model of Jesus' love, is SERVING one another

A second demonstration of Jesus' love was through *serving*. We see this in the context of John 13 by what Jesus did at this final meal. In this vivid and moving account, the disciples have come into the room and reclined at the table. The custom of the oriental households of the day was for the *slave* to wash the feet of the guests as they arrived. The disciples, however, were preoccupied with dreams of elevation and position, and too concerned with themselves to worry about anybody else. Rather than condescend or humiliate themselves by assuming the role of servant, they were all reclined with unwashed feet. I once heard a preacher say, 'They were ready to fight for a throne, not a towel.'

Then, astonishingly, Jesus '...*got up from the table, took off his robe, wrapped a towel around his waist, and poured water into a basin. Then he began to wash the disciples' feet, drying them with the towel he had around him*' (John 13:4-5). Jesus is the embodied Word of God, the Creator of the Universe, and here he was washing the grime of life's walk off his creation's feet. His divine love leaped over the boundaries of class distinctions to serve.

In case they missed the point, '*after washing their feet,*' Jesus '...*put on his robe again and sat down and asked*' them a rhetorical question to explain the significance of what he had just done:

> '*Do you understand what I was doing? You call me "Teacher" and "Lord", and you are right, because that's what I am. And since I, your Lord and Teacher, have washed your feet, you ought to wash one another's feet. I have given you an example to follow. Do as I have done for you. I tell you the truth, slaves are not greater than their master. Nor is the messenger more important than the one who sends the message. Now that you know these things, God will bless you for doing them.*' (John 13:12-17, emphasis mine)

Jesus set the standard for his team. He set an example that they should do as he had done (v. 15). His example became the baseline for how his followers should act toward one another and to people more broadly. Likewise, what the team leader does should become the least for what the team members should do. Based on Jesus' example, a team member should not proudly consider some tasks menial or beneath them for, as Jesus then said, '*slaves are not greater than their master*' (v. 16).

> **Biblical love is not an emotion or sentiment, but is evidenced by exemplary action.**

After washing the feet of his *team*, Jesus urged them (the team members) to emulate his example by also washing the feet of one another (the other team members). One of the embedded lessons here is that if we are to have a true team, we must serve *one another*.

From Jesus' example and words, we also learn that love in a team context is *demonstrated* through serving one another. Biblical love is not an emotion or sentiment, but is evidenced by exemplary action (1 John 3:18). Spiritual love *serves*; it does not desire. Love on a team is others-centred, not self-centred. Love expressed through serving others seeks to make a difference in the other person's life.

Some years ago, I read a moving testimony from Bill Wilson who, at the time, was pastor of the world's largest Sunday School. Located in one of New York's roughest localities, his ministry attracted up to 10,000 children every Saturday afternoon. At the time this story took place, which was back in the mid-1990s, this borough of New York was classified as one of the most violent places on earth. Despite the dangers, Bill Wilson had a fleet of yellow buses that would go out into the surrounding neighbourhoods and transport kids into his facility.

He tells the story that one day a Puerto Rican lady, who had recently found the Lord, came to him to ask if she could serve in some way. She barely spoke English, but through an interpreter expressed that she wanted to do something for Jesus. Bill Wilson didn't know what she could do, but she persisted and basically begged him to be able to do something. Finally, he relented and suggested she get on board one of the buses each Saturday that went out to collect the kids and just love them. She faithfully did this for many months.

After some time, she was drawn to one particular Afro-American boy. Each Saturday, this little boy, accompanied by his older sister, would board the bus on which she served. The young man never spoke a word, yet the Puerto Rican lady would pick him up, sit him on her knee, wrap her arms around him in a loving embrace, and whisper into his ear a few words she'd learned in English, 'Jesus loves you and I love you.' This went on week after week. Though he never verbally responded, the Puerto Rican lady would light up when she saw him each week and shower him with love.

One Saturday afternoon, the little fellow boarded the bus as usual. The lady did what she always did by picking him up, seating him on her knee, enveloping him in her loving arms and whispering in broken English, 'Jesus loves you and I love you.' To her astonishment, this day he turned around, looked her right in the eyes and stammered, 'And…I…love you too,' before throwing his arms around her. It was a beautiful moment.

This happened at 2.30 pm in the afternoon, but at 6.30 pm that night the little boy was found dead. His mother had beaten him up and thrown him out as a piece of trash under the fire escape.

All the little boy had ever known was misery, rejection, abuse and pain, but every Saturday afternoon this Puerto Rican lady with a rudimentary grasp of English was the hands of Jesus, the voice of Jesus and the heart of Jesus. She was like an oasis of love in the desert of this poor boy's misery. She was not a preacher, a singer, or anyone with any profile or prominence, but she *served*. Her serving made a difference in this little boy's life.

Maybe your role on the team seems insignificant, maybe nobody ever encourages or affirms you, or maybe you feel that you haven't got much to offer. If you feel like this, please remember that servant leadership is the highest expression of leadership. In serving others, sometimes in the most seemingly minor ways, you are making a difference in people's lives and you are mirroring Jesus' heart in washing his disciples' feet.

> Love is expressed through serving. Serving makes a difference in people's lives.

Love is expressed through serving. Serving makes a difference in people's lives. Teams need to be knitted together by this kind of serving, which is motivated by love.

Love, based on the model of Jesus' love, is SELF-SACRIFICE for people

A third expression of Jesus' love based on his love for the disciples is seen through his sacrifice for them. In his first letter, the apostle John provides the ultimate definition and description of the type of love we're called to emulate: '*We know what real love is because Jesus gave up his life for us*' (1 John 3:16). The language of '*...Jesus gave up his life for us*' recalls Jesus' own language in John 10 where he portrays himself as the Good Shepherd prepared to lay down his life for his sheep. Love, in this sense, means a readiness and willingness to do anything for other people, no matter what the personal cost. The words '*laid down his life*' indicate that Jesus' love was self-giving, selfless and self-sacrificing.

Therefore, we are called to express sacrificial love to all believers, which includes our fellow team members. John makes a sobering point about the nature of love in the body of Christ. He wrote that we must '...*not merely say that we love each other; let us show the truth by our actions*' (1 John 3:18). David Jackman comments on this verse: 'John exhorts himself, his readers and us not to be loving with the empty evidence of words, but with genuine evidence of actions.'[6] Love must not just be in words, but in deeds. John goes so far as to say that if we see our brother in need and don't do anything, we are deluded and a fraud as a Christian (1 John 3:16-18). True love is evidenced by our selfless, generous acts in helping people.

Our love for one another is a reflection of our love for the Lord. Patrick Morley, known for his writing on topics related to men, is attributed as saying, 'The height of our love for God will never exceed the depth of our love for one another.' John also wrote, '*If someone says, "I love God," but hates a Christian brother or sister, that person is a liar; for if we don't love people we can see, how can we love God, whom we cannot see? And he has given us this command: Those who love God must also love their Christian brothers or sisters*' (1 John 4:20-21). Applying this verse, Jackman again comments: 'Love for the unseen Lord is best expressed not just in words, but in deeds of love towards the Lord's people whom we do see.'[7] If we say that we love God, then we must show it by our loving actions to one another.

It's easy to love our fellow team members with words, '... to express sympathy, to promise to pray, to encourage, but it's our subsequent actions that confirm or deny their truth.'[8] This is the same principle as we see in James 2:14-17 in regard to exercising faith. If faith without deeds is dead, so love without action is inauthentic.

Love should never be just a sentiment or an emotion, but a tangible and practical expression. Jesus' love on the cross was not an empty gesture; it totally transformed our situation. We were: slaves to sin (John 8:34); powerless to do anything about the condition we were in (Romans 5:6, 8); blinded to our predicament and not even aware of our precarious spiritual condition (2 Corinthians 4:4); unworthy, with no merit to deserve what Jesus did for us (Romans 5:7); empty and void of anything that truly satisfied and trapped in endless cycles of meaningless religious observance (1 Peter 1:18-19); and destined for a Christless eternity in hell beyond the grave (Romans 6:23). Nevertheless *'God showed his great love for us by sending Christ to die for us while we were still sinners'* (Romans 5:8). Through the work of the cross, we have been brought: from death in our sins to life in Christ (Ephesians 2:5); from darkness to light (Colossians 1:13); from ignorance to revelation (Ephesians 4:18); from guilt and condemnation to justification and exoneration (Romans 8:1); from unrighteousness to be made righteous; from Satan's kingdom to God's kingdom; from slavery to sin and Satan to redemption (ransom) and liberation; from separation to reconciliation with God (Colossians 1:21-22); from being a child of Satan to being an adopted, blood-bought child of God; from being alienated to being baptised into Christ's body; and from the certainty of punishment in hell to the assurance of future resurrection and eternal life beyond the grave.

As Jesus' loving, sacrificial, substitutionary death on the cross comprehensively and eternally changed our lives, so our love must be demonstrated by selflessly helping others (1 John 4:9-12).

3. WHY WE ARE TO LOVE

Having explored *who* we are to love and *how* we are to love them, we now come to the compelling question of *why* we are to love our fellow team members. Jesus' words in the foundational verses for this chapter, John 13:34-35, provide six compelling reasons.

We are to love one another because, first, Jesus *commanded* us to (John 13:34; 15:12). It is a command. It's not an option,

> The tangible love we have for one another will be persuasive evidence for the Gospel's message.

but an imperative. Therefore, we are to obey him with all our heart.

Secondly, we should love one another because the most natural extension and expression of the redemptive work of Jesus in our hearts should be to show the same love to others. Because he has loved us, we must love one another (1 John 4:19), both on the team and in the broader community of faith. Because our hearts are redeemed and renewed, love is the primary fruit of our new nature (Galatians 5:22).

Loving one another, thirdly, demonstrates that we truly know God. John's first letter, especially in 1 John 2:9-11; cf. 4:7-8, reveals that our love for one another indicates whether we are living in the light (we know God) or remain in the dark (we don't know God). If we're embodying the command to love one another, writes John, the light is in us (1 John 2:8, 10); however, if anyone claims to be a Christ-follower, '...*but hates a Christian brother or sister, that person is still living in darkness*' (1 John 2:9; cf. 2:11; John 12:35).

Fulfilling the command to love one another, fourthly, identifies us as followers of Jesus. After imploring his disciples to love each other based on the way he had loved them, he said, '*Your love for one another will* prove *to the world that you are my disciples*' (John 13:35, emphasis mine). In this verse, Jesus stated that the disciples' love for each other would be a distinguishing mark that they were authentic followers of Jesus. Their love would validate not only their message (Jesus), but them as the messengers (sent by Jesus).

According to John 13:35, fifthly, loving one another is missional. The tangible love we have for one another will be persuasive evidence for the Gospel's message. The command to *'love one another'* cannot be isolated or dislocated from Jesus' overall and overriding mission. Jesus didn't command the disciples to love one another insulated and secluded from the world outside, but as an incarnational and visible demonstration *to* the world. Christians displaying 'Christly love' will, in the words of George Beasley-Murray, '…be a revelation to the world of the reality of Christ's redemption, a witness to the presence and power of the kingdom of God in the midst of the world (v 35; cf. 17:21, 23).'[9] Theologian, philosopher and pastor, Francis Schaeffer wrote that the '…final apologetic which Jesus gave is the observable love of true Christians for true Christians.'[10]

Sixthly, a team's loving relationships, based on Christ's example, would be a model to the world of authentic relationships (John 13:35). The relationships Jesus envisaged in the new community would be new to the world. In other words, the world would never have witnessed or experienced the depth of genuine love as would be seen between the followers of Jesus. If, and only if, we love one another in the way Jesus envisioned, can a lost world starving for a sense of belonging and community see the reality of true community exemplified in the perceptible, demonstrable love we have for one another.

Reflection and discussion from Chapter One: Tangible Love

Personal Reflection:

1. *Who we are to love.* When thinking about the other members of your team, do you genuinely love them? If not, what actions will you take to be more loving toward them? If yes, what can you do to help the team love each other more?
2. *How we are to love.* Thinking about the ways Jesus loved his disciples (i.e. identifying, serving, self-sacrificing), what can you apply to your team from his example?
3. *Why we should love one another.* Reflecting on the six reasons why we should love one another, which one was the most impacting for you? Please write out the reasons why. What will you now endeavour to do to see this become a reality on your team?

Group discussion

What can we do as a team to become a more loving team? If our love for one another on the team is a model to others of authentic relationships, what should we work on to achieve this?

SECTION II

SELFLESS UNITY

CHAPTER 2
Selfless Unity (Part One)

Building on the foundation of love, a second relational principle for an effective team is selfless unity.

To me, the best Bible passage that describes the anatomy of Christian unity is found in Philippians 2:1-4, which reads:

> ¹*Is there any encouragement from belonging to Christ? Any comfort from his love? Any fellowship together in the Spirit? Are your hearts tender and compassionate?* ²*Then make me truly happy by agreeing wholeheartedly with each other, loving one another, and working together with one mind and purpose.*
>
> ³*Don't be selfish; don't try to impress others. Be humble, thinking of others as better than yourselves.* ⁴*Don't look out only for your own interests, but take an interest in others, too.*

Taking the key thoughts from verse two, I propose that a Biblical definition of unity on a team is: 'to agree, love and work together with one heart toward a godly purpose.' Two key words stand out in verse two that encapsulate the essential elements of unity: purpose and oneness.

If the purpose (task) of the team is crystal clear, the big challenge is oneness. So, in this and the next chapter, I will draw out some practical applications from Philippians 2:1-5 and other Scriptures on the ingredients of oneness, which I describe as selfless unity.

1. WORKING TOGETHER

'...working together *with one mind and purpose*' (Philippians 2:2, emphasis mine).

A first action in building unity is 'working together'. There are many aspects of what it means to work together. A number of key words describe and define what working together requires.

Diversity

Working together recognises that no two people on a team are the same. We're all different. There's diversity. In his metaphor of the church being likened to a human body (1 Corinthians 12:12-31; Romans 12:3-8; Ephesians 4:1-16), Paul wrote how each of us has a unique function. Everyone has something to contribute. All the 'members' of the body have equal value. There is diversity but equality (not of responsibility, but of value and necessity). This is not just true in the local church, but also in the context of a team. Therefore, to work together, we need to affirm one another's roles, gifts and contributions as equally valuable and vital as our own.

> Because there is diversity, there needs to be harmony. I once heard a definition of harmony as 'diversity working together in love.'

Harmony

Because there is diversity, there needs to be harmony. Paul urged the Corinthians '...*to live in harmony with each other*'

(1 Corinthians 1:10; cf. 2 Corinthians 13:11). I once heard a definition of harmony as 'diversity working together in love.'

In regard to church leaders being in harmony, Jesus said that: *'If two of you agree here on earth concerning anything you ask, my Father in heaven will do it for you'* (Matthew 18:19, emphasis mine).[11] The word translated 'agree' in this verse is from the Greek word *symphoneo*. The English word 'symphony' derives from the same roots. *Symphoneo* has a general meaning of 'to agree or be in harmony with'. It was used both to describe musical harmony and the fitting together of stones in a building.[12] It shows that when leaders *agree* together, the Lord hears and will answer.

Using the analogy of a symphony, unity in music is not uniformity. The instruments in an orchestra don't all play the one note, but a variety of notes which all harmonise. Similarly, because of our diversity, we all have different parts to play on the team, but it's only when we play in harmony that will we be working together in unity.

All it takes is one team member to be in disharmony (playing the wrong note) and the whole team is in discord. There may be many reasons why a team member may not be in harmony, such as a bad attitude, a lack of commitment, no sense of team, no connection with the team leader, or a duplicitous life. If a team member brings disruption, there won't be clear direction or momentum. Goals may not be achieved and tasks may not be completed effectively, as the following story illustrates.

In the early 2000s, I was invited to join twenty other senior pastors from around the world at a practicum to learn from a fast-growing church in Hawaii. Because it was in Hawaii, I didn't have to pray too hard about whether to go or not! As part of the week together, we had some sports to help build a sense of comradery. One day, we went down to the ocean to race in two large Hawaiian outriggers. One boat was made up exclusively of Americans, while the other was comprised of those of us from other parts of the world. As an Aussie, I am competitive and I particularly like to beat Americans, New Zealanders and the British, so I was determined to try hard.

In each boat was a 'steersperson', who was the individual giving directions to the rowers. It was important that all rowers put their paddles in together and out together, and for the paddles to go through the water at the same speed. When the steersperson yelled 'left', everybody paddled on the left-hand-side, but when he yelled 'right', then we all shifted our paddles to the right-hand-side. However, we had someone on our team who didn't speak English, only Spanish. Every time the steersperson yelled 'left', he would put his paddle in the 'right' until he realised his mistake and would quickly change. Because our Spanish-speaking team member didn't paddle in rhythm with rest of the team, we never moved in a straight line, but swayed from side to side. Consequently, we never really got any momentum and, despite our valiant efforts, the Americans soundly defeated us. Our team was beaten all because one person wasn't in synchronisation with the other members.

This is a great parallel to what happens on teams when a team member is not in harmony or alignment with the rest of the team.

Synergy

If there is diversity and harmony, then a key to working together is synergy, which requires every person to do their part to achieve the team's overall purpose.

Synergy, by definition, means that the sum total of what two or more people can do collectively is greater than what individuals can achieve on their own. The basic concept is that the collective whole (working together) is greater than the sum of its unconnected parts (working separately).

The English word 'synergy' derives from the Greek word *synergos* which, when used in Scripture, refers to 'co-workers' in gospel ministry (Romans 16:3; Philippians 2:25; Colossians 4:11; Philemon 1:24). In other places of Scripture, it can be translated as workers (1 Corinthians 3:9), working together (2 Corinthians 1:24) and partner (2 Corinthians 8:23; cf. Philippians 4:3; 3 John 8). In summary, it means working together. As I quoted in the introduction, Ecclesiastes says that: *'Two people are better off than one, for they can help each other succeed…Three are even better, for a triple-braided cord is not easily broken'* (4:9,12).

> **It is vital that we work together synergistically to accomplish the team's purpose.**

I once shared the speaking at a conference with a successful dentist, who owned many practices across his home province in Canada. He shared that synergy is not just a term used in business or organisations, but a term also used in pharmacology. When two or more pharmaceuticals are administered together, one substance can increase the effect of the others. It has a synergistic effect. He also mentioned that the opposite effect of some drugs is antagonistic; that is, some medicines diminish the effect of another. Antagonism is the opposite of synergism.

The difference between the synergistic and antagonistic effect of some pharmaceuticals made me think of teams. We have to ask ourselves, 'Am I working together with others in such a way that it *increases* the team's overall effectiveness? Or am I having an antagonistic effect on the team that minimises its overall effectiveness?' It is vital that we work *together* synergistically to accomplish the team's purpose.

Vocabulary

If there is diversity, harmony and synergy, then working together is also expressed through the way the team speaks. A unified team *working together* has a unique vocabulary in the way it communicates. Rather than the singular 'I', the language of team is 'we'. Instead of saying 'them', an active team member says 'us'. In the place of the exclusive *'my* vision', a true team player would say the inclusive *'our* vision'.

A disastrous example of a team speaking with disunified voices is that of the twelve men Moses sent out to explore and do reconnaissance on the land of Canaan (Numbers 13:1-20). This chosen team of twelve leaders all saw the same things, but their reports back to the leadership were anything but the same (13:21-24). Ten of the explorers agreed on the beauty and fruitfulness of the land, but were intimidated by the stature of the people and the fortifications of their cities (13:25-29; 31-33). Caleb and Joshua, however, joined their voices in urging the people to immediately take the land, because, from their perspective, it was conquerable (13:30). And, they later added, the Lord was with them, therefore there was no need to be afraid or overawed (13:30; 14:5-9).

This lack of unity among the team affected the whole community, who were not only unsettled and fearful, but wept aloud, protested against their leaders and plotted to appoint new leadership and go back to Egypt (14:1-4). Consequently, the whole generation were forbidden from entering the Promised Land, with the exception of Joshua and Caleb (14:10-12; 22-25). Because the team did not have unity in their vocabulary, the whole generation failed to inherit its destiny.

Mentality

If a team has diversity, harmony, synergy, and the right vocabulary, then a further ingredient of working together is adopting a team *mentality*. This means to be of one mind; that is, to have the right mindset toward one another and the team's purpose.

There are some examples in Scripture of people being of one mind. After the men of the Benjamite city of Gibeah vilely and viciously raped and abused a Levite's concubine—acts which led to her death—men from the other eleven tribes '...*united as one man*...[and] *assembled in the presence of the Lord at Mizpah*' (Judges 20:1). At the gathering, the Levite explained what had happened. In response, '*All the people rose to their feet in unison*...' in their determination to deal with the men of Gibeah (Judges 20:8). They were of one mind.

After Saul's death, thousands of fighting men from all twelve tribes '...*came in battle array*...*with the single purpose of making David the king over all Israel*' (1 Chronicles 12:38). In the early Autumn of the year the exiles returned from their captivity under the Babylonians, then later the Persians, the people '...*assembled in Jerusalem with a unified purpose*' to rebuild the Temple (Ezra 3:1). In both cases, they had a single purpose.

The application here is that a team working together would think like a team, act as a team, pray as a team, work as a team, play as a team, and support each other as a team. This is reminiscent of Benjamin Franklin's renowned quote when signing the American Declaration of Independence, 'We must indeed all hang together, or, most assuredly, we shall all hang separately.'

The well-known quote from Alexandre Dumas' novel, *The Three Musketeers*, sums up this point perfectly: 'All for one; one for all.' That personifies the mentality of a unified team.

Unity is not passive; it requires proactivity.

Proactivity

So, if a team has diversity, harmony, synergy, the right vocabulary and mentality, these are strong indications that the team is proactive in fostering unity.

Unity is not passive; it requires proactivity. It doesn't happen by accident, but through attention and intention. Like all relationships, unity has to be built.

Paul urged the Ephesian believers to '*make every effort to keep yourselves united in the Spirit, binding yourselves together with peace*' (4:3, emphasis mine; cf. Romans 14:19; Hebrews 12:14; 2 Peter 3:14). The words 'make every effort' imply action. It speaks of doing all within our power, doing our best, doing whatever we can, and putting in an effort to work together.

Tying off this first way to build selfless unity, we note that we must *work together*. Working together means we embrace our diversity, flow in harmony, work synergistically, speak the right vocabulary, adopt a team mentality and proactively do and give our best to the team and its task.

2. RESOLVE CONFLICTS QUICKLY AND BIBLICALLY

Back in our study passage (Philippians 2:1-4), Paul asked the Philippians to '*agree wholeheartedly with each other...*' (2:2). Added to this verse is Paul's appeal in 1 Corinthians 1:10 '*... to live in harmony with each other. Let there be no divisions in the church. Rather, be of one mind, united in thought and purpose.*' In this point, we'll discuss how to resolve disagreements in a way that protects unity.

The Merriam Webster dictionary defines *unity* as 'the state of being in full agreement'.[13] Another defines it as the 'opposite of being divided'.[14] Disunity, therefore, would result if there was disagreement and division.

One of the most common causes of disunity and disruption in teams is interpersonal conflict. For a team to foster and protect unity, it is imperative that each person resolves any conflict quickly and biblically. There will inevitably be frictions, misunderstandings or tensions on every team, but the way to preserve unity is to deal with them as quickly as possible in the way prescribed in Scripture. If we don't deal with them quickly and biblically, the conflicts will become like an insidious cancer devouring the vitality and health of the team.

My kids generally were not known for their tidiness, especially the middle one (who shall remain nameless, but she knows who she is). One day, I walked into the room of my youngest son, David, and unsurprisingly the floor was covered in a mess. There were model cars in one section, books sprawled in another, Lego in another corner and an assortment of other toys spread intermittently across the remainder of his floor. I asked David to clean his room. A few minutes later, I walked back into his room and was astonished to find that his floor was spotless. No toys could be seen anywhere. This was not humanly possible. I walked over to his bed and lifted the cover to look under his bed. Sure enough, everything had just been pushed under the bed. In his mind, he had cleaned his room. In my mind, he hadn't. All he'd done was push the mess under his bed, where it wasn't visible.

Tragically, sometimes teams treat conflicts, issues and tensions in the same way David 'cleaned' his room—they brush them under the bed. No-one addresses it. No-one deals with it. As long as it's not spoken about, it's hoped it will just go away. But it *is* still there festering 'under the bed'. Until it is dealt with, it *is* a problem that on a team is the equivalent of a time bomb. It's just a matter of time before the mess under the bed will explode and cause untold problems in the team.

The only preventative way to diffuse the time bomb is to deal with things quickly, talk them through and seek resolution, even if compromises have to be made. Remember that how things are dealt with on the leadership team will filter through to the whole area of ministry. If the team is divisive, the whole group will probably be divisive. If the team has unresolved friction, the group will probably have unresolved friction.

Not dealing with things

My wife Fiona and I have a favourite place to holiday—the Queensland coastal town of Noosa. On one Christmas vacation we were staying at Sunrise Beach, just south of the main centre at Noosa. It was a windy day, so Fiona took her kite down to the beach. She had a particularly long string attached and was enjoying the height to which the kite rose. I asked her if I could have a turn. She looked at me, as only a wife can, with a tentative, rather wary expression and warned, 'Don't let go of the string.'

'Of course not!' I responded, feigning indignation than I would ever be so careless.

Seconds after I took the string, a sudden gust of wind jolted the kite higher. The unexpected force jerked the string out of my grasp. To my horror, the kite flew away down the beach completely out of control. My youngest son, David, and I went running after it, partly to catch it and partly to avoid Fiona's expected castigation. Mercifully, the wind died down and the kite drifted down a few hundred metres away. By the time I got there, the kite was safely resting on a sand dune, but the string was strewn and twisted over dozens of metres. In one section, it was twisted around a thorn bush. In my mind, there was no way we were going to be able to untangle the string from the bush. It would have been laborious, possibly painful work.

Astonishingly, David looked down at his feet and there in the sand was a pair of children's scissors. I thought this was a sign from God. I thought I would cut one side of the kite's string on one side of the bush, then go around the other side and cut the string there also. In this way, the tangled, twisted, entwined string could stay on the bush. I could then join the two untangled lengths of string and the problem would be solved. Doesn't that seem logical?

With scissors in hand, I was just about to make the first cut when Fiona caught up to us. 'Don't do that,' she exclaimed.

'Why not?' I answered in a bewildered tone, thinking it'll be a lot easier than trying to untangle it. After a few more exchanges, Fiona said, 'You treat people exactly the same way.'

In shock, I defensively responded, 'I do not.' She then took the scissors from me and proceeded to unravel the string from the bush.

I began to think about what she'd said, 'You treat people the same way.' What she meant was that whenever someone annoyed, criticised or opposed me, I cut them off, like I intended to do with the string knotted on the thorn bush. Rather than spend time to untangle the issues—real or imagined—I would just cut the person off. I wouldn't ignore or be rude to them, but they no longer had my time, attention, thought or engagement— aside from perfunctory pleasantries.

Her words highlighted a blind spot to me. Until that moment, I'd never seen the pattern in my behaviour before. My eyes were opened. That was over 15 years ago, and I have tried very hard to work at unravelling the entwined string in my relationships ever since. At times, I still find myself being tempted to revert to the 'scissors', but, when working on a team, it is imperative to unravel the twisted string by resolving issues quickly, biblically and thoroughly.

What does the Bible teach about *how* to resolve conflicts?

When a relationship breaks down or you are offended by someone, remember the principle of Matthew 18:15. *'If any believer sins against you, go privately and point out the offense.*

If the other person listens and confesses it, you have won that person back.'

In my book *Inside Out* I address the practicalities of how to resolve conflicts with a fellow team member:

> According to Matthew 18:15, if you are aware of any friction, conflict or hurt with anyone, *you* (the offended person) must take the initiative and *go* to the (offending) person. Jesus did *not* tell his disciples to find sympathetic ears or wait for the offending person to come to them first. On the contrary, he strongly instructed them to have the maturity to *go* themselves. Jesus also said that the motive in seeing the person to discuss the offence must be to reconcile. If you miss this crucial motivation, you've missed the heartbeat of what conflict resolution is about.
>
> Many people carry a 'win/lose' attitude into conflict resolution. If you have a 'win/lose' mindset, the usual result is 'no win', because you're locked into your set positions ('I'm right, you're wrong') and your goal is to win only.[15] You must be prepared to listen objectively and make compromises and concessions for the sake of the relationship.
>
> I will now suggest a step-by-step way to resolve conflict: make contact with the offending person to ask for a face-to-face meeting. If a face-to-face meeting is not practical, then set up a phone call. Don't get into the details of why you want to meet with them in the initial contact. It's best to wait until you meet face-to-

> **Jesus said that the motive in seeing the person to discuss the offence must be to reconcile.**

face. Carefully choose the time and place you'll meet with them. Be sensitive to the other person's circumstances. Avoid meeting at the end of a hard day or if the other person is under pressure.[16] This is critical in conflict resolution. Approach the meeting with a positive attitude. The conflict resolution could be very constructive *if* the other person's behaviour changes as a result, and your relationship remains intact or is restored. Above all, initiating contact to resolve a conflict is pleasing to God, and it will keep your life free from offence and bitterness. Pray a lot about the forthcoming meeting. Ask God for his peace. Ask for a good outcome. Ask for a preserved or restored relationship. Rehearse what you're going to say, how you're going to say it and anticipate their possible responses. This will help you think more clearly and respond in measured tones.

Ensure the environment for where you're meeting with them is conducive for a conversation of this nature. Avoid places where there are lots of distractions. When you meet with them, welcome them and thank them for coming. Once you get through the pleasantries, get straight to the issue. If you're feeling anxious or it is a tense atmosphere, have a drink of water, otherwise your mouth may go dry, or silently take some deep breaths to lower your emotional temperature. Begin by saying *why* you called the meeting. 'I have certain feelings about what you said or did yesterday. Could you please help me to understand why? This is how I interpreted what you said.' Explain *why* you're upset and why you feel the way you do. Then listen objectively. There are always two sides to a story. Some say there are actually three sides: theirs, mine and the truth.

At the outset of the conversation, state that your goal is to sort things out and move on in the relationship.

Say things like, 'I don't want anything between us. I don't want any negative feelings. I don't want there to be any misunderstandings.' Keep your cool and listen to everything they say without interruption or judgment. Control your tone of voice, tempo, volume and, importantly, your *non-verbals*, such as your facial expression and body language.[17] Don't accuse with your voice or eyes, but show that you're listening by maintaining eye contact. Keep talking through the issues until you feel you have peace and some sense of resolution. Say whatever apologies are appropriate. Determine how it can be avoided in the future. Maybe work out some action steps. Pray for one another. Affirm each other and the relationship. Conclude the discussion.

If, however, you're not getting anywhere, maybe postpone the encounter, go for a short walk, or consider getting another person as a mediator. If it still deteriorates and there's no resolution or reconciliation, senior church leaders will have to be involved (Matthew 18:16-20).[18]

In applying this to our lives, here are a few applications for resolving conflicts:

- Do your best to keep all your relationships clean and clear of offence and tension;
- Don't let things foment or fester in your heart or mind;
- Maintain a forgiving spirit (more about that in chapter seven);
- If you hear of any other criticism, bad attitude or division, urge the instigators or agitators to put relationships right and sort things out as soon as possible;
- Lovingly correct and reason with divisive people (Titus 3:10; 2 Timothy 2:22-26), which may involve refuting what they say and reiterating the importance of unity;

- Remember the guiding principle of Ephesians 4:26: '*...do not let the sun go down while you are still angry.*' Don't go to sleep with unresolved anger in your heart.

It's been my observation that most problems on a team generally stem from three things: misunderstanding, misinterpretation and/or misinformation. Meeting face-to-face quickly may resolve issues before they get out of hand and circumvent unnecessary emotion or anger.

Many years ago, a friend of mine was running the combined youth gatherings for his denomination. One night they had an event at his church where many youth groups from other churches joined in. From all reports it was an incredible night.

One young man from another church saw his pastor after the Sunday morning service the following day. After being asked how the youth service went, the young man reported, 'Pastor, it was a great night. They had flashing lights, great music, a smoke machine and a funny speaker.'

The next day my friend—the organiser of the youth event—received a scathing letter from the pastor of the other church who had received the report from his young parishioner. The pastor was indignant and affronted that my friend would have a 'cigarette dispenser' in his church! When the young man had said 'smoke machine', by which he meant a dry ice machine that produces smoke-like fog for effect, the pastor had thought he meant a vending machine that dispenses packets of cigarettes.

> **It's been my observation that most problems on a team generally stem from three things: misunderstanding, misinterpretation and/or misinformation.**

My friend immediately rang the pastor who had written the letter and explained the misunderstanding. The pastor was incredibly apologetic and embarrassed by his mistake. It could have been avoided if the offended pastor had simply picked up the phone, rang my friend and calmly sought an explanation. Instead, an unnecessary waste of time and emotion ensued, which all stemmed from a misinterpretation.

Similarly, most problems on teams could be avoided or mitigated if we would stop taking offence so quickly, whether by internalising or exploding, and do what Jesus told us to: go and sort things out. Harbouring offence is damaging to us personally and to the team.

Agree wholeheartedly

So far in this point we've looked at how to agree together by resolving conflicts. That said, Paul did not just say to agree, but to agree *wholeheartedly*. In other words, to agree with the right attitude.

Agreeing wholeheartedly means that we are *not half-hearted* in the sense of it being a begrudging agreement; that is, we'll outwardly comply and fit in, but inwardly we're critical and would distance ourselves if things didn't pan out as expected. I've heard people say, 'I'm doing this to keep everyone happy, but I'm not happy about it.' That is not wholehearted agreement, but a negative attitude that will undermine unity. Alternatively, may we agree with a positive and supportive attitude, though this may firstly involve having some frank conversations to resolve any underlying concerns. Added to this is the necessity to guard our personal attitudes toward the other team members, especially those whose opinion we may not share. Most disunity begins with a bad attitude, but it can be solved by a change of attitude.

3. BE OTHERS-CENTRED (not self-centred)

The story is told of a salesman who called a particular home. A young boy answered the phone by saying, 'Hello', in a barely audible whisper. The chirpy salesman said, 'Hello, young man, may I speak with your mother?' 'No', whispered the little chap, 'she's busy.' The unperturbed salesman responded, 'Oh, ok, may I speak with your father?' The youngster replied, 'No, he's busy, too.'

Trying to stay calm, the salesman then asked, 'Is there anybody else there?' Without missing a beat, the boy quietly answered, 'Yes, the policeman is here.' This surprised the salesman, but he kept his tone neutral by asking, 'Well, may I speak with the policeman please?' To his shock, the boy replied, 'No, he's busy too.' There was a moment of silence as the salesman worked out what he would say next. He was getting a little ruffled. Keeping his voice moderate, he tried another time, 'Is there *anybody* else there?' 'Yes', said the little boy, 'the fire officer is here.' 'Well, may I please speak with him?' asked the frustrated salesman. 'No', said the boy, 'he's busy too.'

Now exasperated, the salesman lost his composure and blurted out a final question, 'Well, what are they all doing?' The child calmly answered in a hushed voice, 'They're looking for me!'

Sadly, some team members have the same attitude as this little boy—it's all about *me*. But, what we're about to discover, is that for a team to relate and function well, we cannot have a self-centred attitude. The team is not about me.

As we've been diving deeper into Philippians 2:2-4, we've seen that to build unity, we need to work and agree together, but then Paul challenged his Philippian readers not to look after their own selfish interests, '...*but take an interest in others*' (2:4). In a similar vein, in Romans he wrote that Christians should '*honour one another above yourselves*' (Romans 12:10).

What we draw from these verses is that if unity is to be attained, we must not be self-centred. Instead, a guiding principle for teams is for each team member to be *others-centred*. But how do we do this? The remainder of Philippians 2:2-3 provides some practical principles: *'Don't be selfish; don't try to impress others. Be humble, thinking of others as better than yourselves. Don't look out only for your own interests, but take an interest in others, too.'*

There are three important principles from these verses we need to apply if we are to be others-centred: don't be selfish, be humble, and show an interest in others. We'll now unpack each one.

Don't be selfish

Philippians 2:3 opens with a very strong directive: *'Don't be selfish'*. These words speak of the need to have the right motive in why we do what we do on the team. Paul then names a clearly negative motive: '…*don't try to impress others.*' In other words, don't be self-seeking, simply doing things to draw attention to yourself or to receive recognition from people. This implies that we're doing it for ourselves, not others. Self-centred people do things for their own vanity, own recognition, own glory or to puff up their ego. We, however, are instructed not be selfish, so that we can cultivate unity.

Be humble

Instead of being selfish, Paul urged the Philippians to *'be humble'* by *'thinking of others better than yourselves'* (2:3).

Generally, Scriptural references to humility are in regard to a person's relationship with, or attitude toward, God. Many significant people in the Bible are identified as humble, namely: Moses (Numbers 12:3); Daniel (Daniel 10:12); Mary (Luke 1:48); Paul (Acts 20:19) and Jesus (Matthew 11:29). Jesus is the embodiment of humility through his incarnation, when he emptied himself of the divine privileges and position in heaven to come in human form to serve. He humbly submitted himself in obedience to his Father's will to die a criminal's death on the cross to provide redemption (Philippians 2:7-8).

> 'Humility is not thinking less of yourself, but thinking of yourself less.'
>
> CS Lewis

There are two ways we can attain humility. We can either humble ourselves before the Lord (Proverbs 3:34; James 4:6, 7, 10; 1 Peter 5:5-6)[19] or be humbled by the Lord (Luke 14:11; 18:14).[20]

Being humble begins with having a right estimation of ourselves in relation to God. The Message paraphrase of Romans 12:3 reads, *'The only accurate way to understand ourselves is by what God is and by what he does for us, not by what we are and what we do for him.'* Rick Warren paraphrased some thoughts of CS Lewis by stating that, 'Humility is not thinking less of yourself, but thinking of yourself less.'[21] Or, to paraphrase John Haggai's description, humility is recognising that in ourselves we are nothing, but in God we are everything.[22] Therefore, we should *'...humble* [ourselves] *before God'* (James 4:6), and maintain a child-like trust, dependence and obedience to him (Matthew 18:1-4).

But Scripture also teaches us to be humble in our attitude to one another (Ephesians 4:2; Titus 3:2). Peter instructed his readers to *'...serve each other in humility...* (1 Peter 5:5), and Paul wrote that since , *'...God chose you to be the holy people he loves, you must clothe yourselves with...humility...',* among other qualities (Colossians 3:12).

Paul's letter to the Roman believers articulates practical ways in which we show a humble attitude toward others. Beginning with 12:3, the attitude of humility we need to embrace is further explored in the remainder of the chapter (Romans 12:4-21). The following is a list of principles drawn from these verses that spell out how we show humility to one another:

- By recognising we are just one part of Christ's body and that we *'all belong to each other'* (v. 5);
- By not *'enviously or pridefully comparing ourselves with each other, or trying to be something we aren't'* (v.5, MSG);
- By exercising our God-given gifts to serve others (vv. 6-8);
- By loving others sincerely, not superficially or by faking it (vv. 9-10);
- By helping people in practical ways whenever there is a need or opportunity (v. 13);
- By showing hospitality, inviting people into your home (v. 13);
- By empathising with others in times of happiness and hardship (v. 15);
- By *'living in harmony with each other'*, getting on with everyone (vv. 16, 18);
- By not showing partiality or discrimination, but mixing with people who are regarded, in the eyes of the culture, as nobodies, of a lower social status (class or caste) or inferior (v. 16);
- By living an honourable life (v. 17);
- By not hitting back or getting even with those who hurt or hinder us, but always responding with love, allowing God to bring about his justice in his time (vv. 14, 19-20).

Early in the 2000s, when I was pastoring a church in Brisbane, I was invited to Shanghai, China, to meet with the top leaders of a large network of house churches which were seeking someone to help them do leadership training. A colleague and I flew there and, after a 24-hour door-to-door trip, checked into the hotel which had been designated for the meeting. The meeting was scheduled for the next day. No sooner had we begun to unpack, than there was a knock on the door. I opened the door and a young Chinese man said in good English, 'They're ready for you.' I asked, 'Who is ready for us?' 'All the leaders,' he replied, 'they're waiting for you upstairs.' 'But I thought the meeting wasn't until tomorrow?' I responded. 'For security reasons,' he explained, 'they all came a day early. They are waiting for you now.' Then he told us the room number. We told him that we needed a few minutes to freshen up, but promised to come as soon as possible.

A little while later, we went to the nominated room, knocked on the door and waited. Seconds later, the door opened to reveal a room packed with about 20 men of all ages. All the chairs had been laid out in preparation for the meeting. We were warmly greeted, though we didn't know anyone at all. The eldest man in the room was seated in the middle. As I came further into the room, he got out of his seat and gestured for me to take *his* seat. I soon discovered that the man who offered his seat was the founder and presiding 'uncle' (leader) of the network of house churches. At the time, they had a membership of around ten-million people spread over many provinces in southern China. I found out later that he had suffered greatly through persecution. Aside from terms of imprisonment, his legs had been broken by the police to try and stop him from moving about in his ministry. Consequently, he walked with bowed legs. I felt so humbled that a man of his leadership stature and seniority, who had suffered greatly for his faith, would give his seat for me—a relative nobody from nowhere. His humility and servant heart profoundly touched me. To me, he embodied what it means to put others before ourselves.

Show an interest in others

In addition to not being selfish but being humble, Philippians 2:4 clearly states that we are not to *'...look out only for your own interests, but take an interest in others, too.'* This means not just thinking about ourselves, but consciously thinking about others.

The New Testament contains many 'one another' statements which portray how we are to show an interest in others:

- love one another (John 13:34-35; 1 John 3:11);
- accept one another (Romans 15:7);
- be devoted to one another (Romans 12:10);
- honour one another (Romans 12:10);
- live in harmony with one another (Romans 12:16; 1 Peter 3:8);
- don't judge (or condemn) one another (Romans 14:13);
- build up (edify) one another (Romans 14:19);
- instruct (teach) one another (Romans 15:14);
- agree with one another (1 Corinthians 1:10);
- care equally for one another (1 Corinthians 12:25);
- greet one another (2 Corinthians 13:12);
- serve one another (Galatians 5:13);
- don't devour one another with negative words (Galatians 5:15);
- be patient with one another (Ephesians 4:2);
- be kind and compassionate to one another (Ephesians 4:32);
- speak to one another with psalms, hymns and spiritual songs (Ephesians 5:19);
- submit to one another (Ephesians 5:21);
- forgive one another (Colossians 3:13);

- admonish one another with all wisdom (Colossians 3:16);
- comfort one another (1 Thessalonians 4:18);
- build up (encourage) one another (1 Thessalonians. 5:11);
- live in peace with one another (1 Thessalonians 5:13);
- consider how we may spur one another toward love and good deeds (Hebrews 10:24).

As we stop being so self-centred, adopt a humble attitude toward God and one another, and purposefully show an interest in each other, we develop the quality of being others-centred.

Reflection and discussion from Chapter Two: Selfless Unity (Part One)

Personal Reflection:

1. *Working together.* Thinking about the key words from this point (i.e. diversity, harmony, synergy, vocabulary, mentality and proactivity), what one was most relevant to you? Please write out the reason why. What do you need to specifically address to work more relationally with others on the team?
2. *Resolve conflicts quickly and biblically.* Please reflect on your relationships with the other team members. Do you harbour any wrong attitudes, offence or hurt toward anyone? If so, what will you do you today to work on these feelings and attitudes? Do you need to put anything right with anyone? If so, please write out what process you'll follow to do so.
3. *Be others-centred.* Please write out what you will do from today to be a more others-centred team member. Who do you need to get to know better? Please write out how you will endeavour to do so?

Group discussion

How, in practical terms, can we develop a greater sense of unity as a team? Let's identify the ways in which we're not working together well, then pinpoint ways in which we can improve (or remedy) any such problems.

CHAPTER 3
Selfless Unity (Part Two)

We're half way through six principles necessary to develop selfless unity. In the previous chapter we looked at (1) working together, (2) resolving conflicts and (3) being others-centred. We'll now cover the remaining three attitudes and actions.

4. ADOPT THE ATTITUDE OF A SERVANT LEADER

Having worked our way through Philippians 2:2-4, Paul provides the pre-eminent example of '...*thinking of others as better than yourselves...*' by highlighting the self-emptying of Jesus. He wrote that we should '...*have the same attitude that Christ Jesus had...taking the very nature of a servant...*' (2:5,7).

When Paul addressed the factions in the Corinthian church, he reasoned with them that they should not be polarised around personalities, namely Apollos or Paul. He called them 'worldly', mere infants in Christ, because there were jealousies, quarrels and factions in their community (1 Corinthians 3:1-4). He wrote, '*What, after all, is Apollos! And what is Paul? Only servants, through whom you came to believe—as the Lord has assigned to each his task... For we are God's fellow workers; you are God's field, God's building*' (1 Corinthians 3:5, 9). Paul regarded himself as the Lord's servant doing what God had assigned for him to do. Similarly, if we are to foster true unity, then we must adopt a similar mindset and see ourselves doing our part on the team as a servant of the Lord.

Jesus had to correct the disciples' misconception and misunderstanding of spiritual leadership. Two gospels record an incident where James and John–the two sons of Zebedee– approached Jesus seeking appointment to senior roles of prominence and power in Jesus' future kingdom (Matthew 20:20-28; Mark 10:35-45). It appears they were interpreting Jesus' kingdom politically, hierarchically and selfishly. When the ten other disciples heard about James and John's request, they were *'indignant'* with them (Matthew 20:24). In addition, other places in the gospels disclose that there had been a fermenting debate about which of them was the greatest (Luke 9:46-48; cf. Mark 9:33-37). Evidently, there was a problem in the team because of a wrong attitude toward the nature of leadership. Jesus seized the moment by bringing corrective teaching on the true measure of greatness and the nature and motivation of spiritual leadership (Matthew 20:25-28).

In Matthew 20:25-28, Jesus drew a clear contrast between authority and greatness in the eyes of the prevailing culture, to authority and greatness in the eyes of the Kingdom. As we examine his words more closely, we see a number of parallels and lessons for contemporary Christian leaders.

'But among you it will be different.' (v. 26)

The words, *'But among you it will be different'*, are a call to a different way of thinking–a 'Kingdom' way of thinking. Through these words Jesus called for a definitive demarcation and distinction between Gentile thinking and Kingdom thinking. In other words, the concept of leadership in the prevailing culture (what Jesus referred to as the *'rulers of this world'*) must not permeate or distort the kingdom mindset of leadership. Spiritual leaders must think differently, as Jesus was about to explain.

'Instead whoever wants to be a leader among you must be your servant, and whoever wants to be first among you must become your slave...' (vv. 26-27)

In graphic and unmistakable contrast to how the world views greatness and practises leadership, Jesus called his disciples to demonstrate true greatness and kingdom leadership by adopting the attitude of a servant leader. Michael Green comments,

> Greatness in the world is determined by status; in the kingdom by function. In the world greatness is shown by *ruling*; in the kingdom by *serving*. In the world's eyes the great are those who can order others about; in the kingdom they are those who endure hard times and injustice without complaining.[23]

The motivation of a spiritual leader is not power, popularity, prominence or prestige. Rather, as defined by Jesus, it is selflessness, service and sacrifice. The important thing to God (and should be to us also) is not the *position* a leader holds, but the *service* a leader offers.

Many years ago, in the mid 1980s, when I was a youth pastor with a mullet (something I cringe about now), I was standing at the front of the meeting hall after a youth service. One of the young men in the youth group came to speak with me. 'I would like to lead the songs one night,' he cockily proclaimed. I looked at him and said something along the lines of, 'Well, Rob (not his real name), we'll consider that, but right now would you please go around and pick up all the mess

> **The motivation of a spiritual leader is not power, popularity, prominence or prestige. Rather it is selflessness, service and sacrifice.**

that the young people have left.' There were loads of papers and stuff littered all over the meeting hall. 'No!' he exclaimed, 'That's not my ministry. I want to lead songs.' I momentarily looked at him, somewhat stunned by his response, before asking again, 'Rob, would you please help out cleaning up the hall?' Again, he indignantly retorted, 'No! That's not what I am called to do. I am called to lead songs.' I then went on to try to explain that he couldn't just have a public role leading songs if he wasn't prepared to serve behind the scenes. I'm not sure he understood the point I was trying to make.

We must not be like Rob and just desire the up-front roles on the team without also having the willingness to serve behind the scenes. Serving in the little things, in the mundane tasks, without recognition, without applause or accolades, in secret, is the place where authentic servant leaders are formed and fashioned.

Since joining World Outreach, I have been on a massive learning-curve of understanding the intricacies and complexities of cultures. I have visited Bangladesh on many occasions, mainly to conduct leadership development seminars. Our Bangladeshi facilitator runs a highly effective ministry that impacts thousands of lives. For security reasons, I can't publish their names or details of their work.

Several years ago, we had a gathering of our global personnel in Thailand. I was having a meal with the team from Bangladesh. I was thirsty and went to get a drink from the buffet. As I stood, I asked, 'Who else would like a drink?' Everyone was quite reluctant, but eventually one or two said, 'Yes, thank you.' I returned with a number of glasses of drink and distributed them to those who asked. They all sat around quietly, heads bowed slightly, nobody spoke. I thought something was wrong, but wasn't sure how to approach it.

Eventually, the team leader, who was one of the few who could speak English said, 'Bruce, the group don't know what to say. You are a conference speaker. You brought *them* a drink. They feel very humbled and embarrassed. It should be us bringing *you* a drink.'

At the time, my response was that it was the least I could do. I hadn't yet fully understood the hierarchical nature of their culture or what missiologists call the power/distance ratio that exists in some cultures.

Christians in Bangladesh are a persecuted minority. The wages of this particular ministry barely kept them above the poverty line. They were doing an extraordinary work in their nation. They were dedicated, sacrificial, spiritual and loving people. It was actually an honour for *me* to get drinks for them. It showed me how expressions of servanthood can build bonds and cement the team.

The key lesson from these words of Jesus is to foster a servant heart to exercise true kingdom leadership.

'For even the Son of Man came not to be served but to serve others and give his life as a ransom for many' (v. 28).

As the perfect example and embodiment of not being first but 'servant' (vv. 26-27), Jesus referred to the *purpose* of his incarnation, life and ministry. He had not come to *be* served, but *to* serve (not status, but function). In addition, he came to *'give away his life in exchange for the many who are held hostage'* (MSG) to sin's slavery, Satan's tyranny and eternal death. Through his sacrifice and selflessness, Jesus came to bring people into right standing and relationship with God, which is a radically new dimension of living.

In summing up and applying this point to Christian leaders, true greatness in God's kingdom is not position, dominance or ordering others about, but selflessly doing whatever is

> True greatness and authentic spiritual leadership is servant leadership.

necessary to help people to fulfil God's purpose for their lives.

True greatness and authentic spiritual leadership is servant leadership. There's nothing wrong with aspiring to become a bigger and better leader. What I'm trying to emphasise is the importance of our *motivation*, which should be to use whatever leadership position we hold to *serve* others.

To build unity, our focus must not be on the *position* we hold, but on the *service* we offer. Let's recognise and fulfil our unique place on the team with a servant attitude and a motivation to serve others.

Diverging from Philippians 2:2-4, we'll now look at two other biblical ways in which we can promote selfless unity.

5. PRAY FOR AND WITH EACH OTHER

A fifth way we can foster and protect unity as a team is to pray for and with each other. This is both private prayer (praying *for*) and public prayer (praying *with*). Let's examine both these expressions of prayer.

Praying *for* each other

The principle here is to consciously and conscientiously pray *for* those with whom we serve. Here are some ideas of things to pray for:

Your leaders…

- Pray that your leaders and pastors would be shepherds who vigilantly and compassionately watch over, and care for, the flock under their care (Acts 20:28; Hebrews 13:17-18; 1 Peter 5:2-4)

- Pray that the pastors and elders who preach and teach God's word may do so boldly, wisely and with discernment (2 Timothy 2:15, 4:2; Colossians 1:28)
- Pray that the church leaders would equip and mobilise people in their areas of gifting to do God's work so the local church may be built up (Ephesians 4:12)
- Pray that your leaders would be strong in the grace that God provides and not succumb to temptations that could disqualify them (2 Timothy 2:1)
- Pray that God's grace would enable them to carry the stresses and weight of their responsibilities (2 Corinthians 11:28)
- Pray that your leaders would multiply themselves by intentionally investing in and discipling emerging leaders (2 Timothy 2:2)
- Pray that your leaders would endure the hardships and adversities of leadership with the resolve of a soldier in combat, the discipline of an athlete and the hard work of a farmer (2 Timothy 2:3-6)
- Pray that your pastors, leaders, teachers and preachers would be centred on the Gospel of Jesus Christ (2 Timothy 2:8-10)
- Pray that the church's decision-makers may have wisdom in the decisions they have to make and clarity in the vision they set (Acts 6:3; 13:1-3; 15:6, 28)
- Pray for your leader's marriage and family life to be healthy, godly and exemplary (1 Timothy 3:4-5, 3:12; cf. Titus 1:6)

One another (on the team)…

- Pray specifically for each person on the team (Luke 22:31-32; 1 Thessalonians 5:25; Colossians 4:2-4; Ephesians 6:19-20)

- Pray for oneness—unity of mind and heart—on the team (John 17:21-23)
- Pray that the team would genuinely love each other and be in authentic relationship (John 13:34)
- Pray that the team's model and demonstration of love would be a witness to the broader non-Christian community regarding the gospel message (John 13:35)
- Pray that each team member would grow in Christlike character and conduct (2 Corinthians 3:18) and bear the fruit of the Holy Spirit (Galatians 5:22-23)
- Pray for the Holy Spirit's power to strengthen each team member's inner being (Ephesians 3:16)
- Pray that each one would live a life of active faith and that each person's faith would increase (2 Peter 1:5-7)
- Pray for each person to exercise their God-given gifts and talents (Romans 12:6-8; 1 Corinthians 12:7-11; 1 Peter 4:10-11)
- Pray for the team to be undistracted, and to remain focused and fruitful in their assigned task (Nehemiah 4:6, 21-23)
- Pray for everyone to have a selfless, others-centred sense of community on the team (Philippians 2:3-4)

Praying *with* each other

Praying with each other is another way of saying praying together as a team. Scripture shows the value of such unified prayer.

In the Old Testament, we read of God's response to Solomon's prayer of dedication of the newly built Temple. The Lord promised that, in the event of national calamity, *'…if my people who are called by my name will humble themselves and pray and seek my face and turn from their wicked ways, then I will hear from heaven and will forgive their sin and heal their land'* (2 Chronicles 7:14). At a time of crisis, God promised that *if* his people would gather together in the Temple and offer heartfelt prayer with a humble and contrite attitude, he would give attention and intervention to their supplication.

> Unified prayer brings answers to prayer.

Over 100 years later, Jehoshaphat called the people of Judah together to pray and fast when vastly outnumbered and threatened by an alliance of armies (2 Chronicles 20:1-4). The outcome of their united prayer was that the Lord defeated the enemy (v. 22).

The same pattern is seen in the New Testament. In Acts 1:14, the faithful believers prayed together in anticipation of the Holy Spirit's coming. The following chapter records that, while they were praying, the Holy Spirit was poured out upon them (2:1-4). Later, in Acts 4, the early church prayed in the face of opposition and were filled afresh with the Spirit and enabled to proclaim the gospel boldly (4:31). Acts 12 records the story of King Herod having Peter arrested to please the Jews, *'…but the church was earnestly praying to God for him'* (v. 5), resulting in Peter's miraculous release. Unified prayer brings answers to prayer.

Ultimately, true unity is a work of the Holy Spirit. As someone has well said, 'The team that prays together, stays together.'

6. SUPPORT THE TEAM LEADER AND HIS/HER VISION

To nurture unity in a team, each member needs to exhibit an inward and outward attitude of respect and honour toward their team leader. This does not mean idealising or idolising them, but respecting and honouring them.

Before exploring some of the positive and practical ways in which we can support our team leaders, here is a brief list from

Scripture of some team members who did *not* support their leader. Miriam was punished with leprosy after criticising her younger brother Moses' interracial marriage and questioning whether God would only speak through him and not through her or Aaron (Numbers 12). Korah and his family were swallowed up by the earth after rebelling against Moses and seeking to lead a breakaway group back to Egypt (Numbers 16:1-3, 32-33). Joab and his family were cursed by David after Joab had vengefully murdered Abner, who had been sent in peace after defecting to David (2 Samuel 3:28-29). Absalom died in humiliating circumstances after unsuccessfully trying to usurp the throne from his father, David (2 Samuel 18:9, 15). Joab, then Israel's army commander, was the one who murdered Absalom against King David's strict orders (2 Samuel 18:10-14). In the end, Joab was executed for aligning with Adonijah rather than Solomon, who wanted to *'remove the guilt of Joab's senseless murders'* of Abner and Amasa (1 Kings 2:31-34). Judas, though chosen to be an apostle, became an apostate, and ultimately killed himself after his betrayal of Jesus (Matthew 27:3-5).

With these sobering examples as a warning, here are three towering Biblical examples of team members who *did* support their leaders. Each of them provides invaluable lessons we can apply to our team leader.

First, when Jonathan boldly rallied his armour-bearer to go attack a Philistine outpost, the armour-bearer responded, *'Do all that you have in mind. Go ahead; I am with you heart and soul'* (1 Samuel 14:7). The role of Jonathan's armour-bearer was not only to arm him with the weapons he needed to fight, but to cover his back and finish off the Philistines which Jonathan had struck down. This is a great picture of the attitude we need to have toward our team leader. We cover their back and we stand with them *'heart and soul.'*

Secondly, after Saul's death, and David's anointing as King at Hebron, there was a period of instability as some of Saul's former soldiers had not yet shown their true allegiance. While David was in his stronghold at Ziklag, thirty Benjaminite men came to defect to him. Because Saul was from the tribe of Benjamin, David was initially suspicious of their motives and intentions. Though cautiously willing to unite with them, David, in essence, asked how he could trust them. At this point, the Holy Spirit moved upon Amasai, the chief of the thirty, who prophetically declared, *'We are yours, O David! We are with you, O son of Jesse! Success, success to you, and success to those who help you, for your God will help you'* (1 Chronicles 12:18). The Holy Spirit had moved their hearts to recognise and affirm David as their God-appointed and anointed leader. Further, the Spirit touched their hearts to express their allegiance and support for his leadership (*'we are yours…we are with you'*) and their desire for him, and those who supported him, to succeed in leadership with God's help (*'success to you, and success to those who help you, for God will help you'*). David was then reassured that the defecting Benjaminites were fully supportive of him and his leadership.

The application for us on our teams is to do and say whatever we can to make our leaders effective in their role.

A third example is found on the Israelites' perilous journey from Egypt toward the Promised Land, when the Amalekites came to attack them at Rephidim (Exodus 17:8-15). Moses instructed Joshua to marshal the troops to engage the threat the next day. While the Israelite forces fought the Amalekites, Moses went onto a nearby hill to intercede by raising his hands (17:11). As long as his hands were up, Joshua and his forces prevailed against the Amalekites, but when Moses' arms tired, the advantage in the battle swung to the Amalekites. After some time, Moses' hands naturally became weary and heavy, so some of his support team sat Moses down on a large rock and two of his assistants, Aaron and Hur, came along beside him and each held up one of his hands. Supported by his team, Moses' hands *'...remained steady till sunset. So Joshua overcame the Amalekite army with the sword'* (Exodus 17:12-13).

Bishop TD Jakes insightfully notes that, in this story, there are some leaders who have their hands *on*, other leaders have their hands *under*, while some leaders have their hands *up*. Those with their hands *on* were Joshua and his troops in the valley, which Jakes equates to those on the frontline of ministry. Those with their hands *under* are the team members whose role is to support the team leader. Those with their hands *up* are the team leaders who carry the weight of oversight and responsibility. The lesson of this story is that the more we can lift up the hands of the team leader, especially the senior leader, the more likely we are to experience victory in our ministry.

> The more we can lift up the hands of the team leader, especially the senior leader, the more likely we are to experience victory in our ministry.

In practical terms, if we are to hold up the hands of our leaders, we need to do all we can to relieve them of unnecessary burdens, and not just draw from them, but pour into them. In addition, let's endeavour to encourage them, pray for them, defend them, watch out for them, and speak well of them publicly and privately.

Some years ago, I was doing some quite heavy work in my backyard. I wasn't looking forward to it because I really don't enjoy gardening or manual labour. Unknown to me, our youth pastor at the time organised a group of well-built young men to come around to my home and do all the heavy work for me. I was really touched and felt that these guys were, in a sense, holding up my arms.

The danger of disunity

Unity often centres around a purpose, a common cause or goal. If the purpose and vision of the group are clearly defined, they become unifying factors. Supporting our leaders, therefore, also means that we wholeheartedly embrace, believe in and support the leader's vision.

If you cannot, with good conscience or attitude, *fully* support your team leader's vision, then seriously consider stepping away from the team. But please do this prayerfully, slowly and advisedly. If you have a diametric view, can't embrace the leader's vision, or have philosophical or theological differences, then please take the following steps: search your heart to ensure your attitudes are right, reflect on the nature of your concerns to determine whether they are really that serious or not, talk through any issues with the relevant people and seek the counsel of wise leaders. If necessary, go to the team leader in private and courteously seek to discuss your concerns. If, after due process and wise counsel, you still can't find resolution to your apprehensions, graciously and respectfully resign and look for another place to serve. Otherwise, the issues may ferment in your heart, your attitude may deteriorate and you may potentially cause division.

There is a difference, however, between being unable to support a leader's vision and being unable to support the leader. Being unable to support the leader, as distinct from her/his vision, is a completely different proposition. We have to be able to discern the difference. Even then, if you're unable to support the leader because of issues in their character or integrity, then you should respectfully resign. But if the issues are along the lines of a personality clash, their leadership style, their lack of experience, or a lack of personal engagement or connection, then my encouragement would be to stay involved and be part of their support team as they develop and grow.

> In my experience, disunity would be the number one reason why teams fail, even more so than a lack of competence.

Beware the danger of disunity. Disunity causes division. The word 'division' derives from both Latin and French. The Latin word *divis* is a mathematical term as in 'division' or 'divisible' and means to separate into parts. Others simply note that the word 'di' means 'two' (or more), so the word division can mean 'two visions'. Division is destructive on a team. In my experience, disunity would be the number one reason why teams fail, even more so than a lack of competence. Disunity is on a team leads to the equivalent of a shipwreck.

FINAL STORY

To illustrate this final thought of unity being indispensable to accomplish a God-given vision, the story is told of a young farming family in the wheat belt of Kansas. Their three-year-old son had uncharacteristically wandered off beyond the boundaries of their farmstead. In every direction, there were hundreds of hectares of wheat fields. After hours of fruitless searching, the near-frantic parents rang the emergency services, then all their immediate family, friends and neighbouring properties. As parties of people began to arrive, the local fire officer, who had assumed the role of search coordinator, sent them off in different directions, carefully designating the boundaries.

By sunset there was no trace of the boy. Undeterred, every available torch or source of light was seconded so the search could continue. The temperature plummeted but not their determination. As they regrouped at 1.00 am to discuss the next step, one of the farmers known for his pragmatism said, 'Look, he's three. He can't have gone too far—one or two miles at the most. All I can suspect is that the little fellow got tired and laid down to sleep. We've obviously walked right past him. Let's join hands and walk through every field until we find him.' This met with unanimous support. They joined hands to form a human chain and systematically walked through the fields.

As they reached one of the last fields within the assigned radius, it was nearly dawn and barely above freezing. After walking just a few metres, someone's torch identified the unmistakable shape of a small body. Those nearest rushed over as quickly as possible. A neighbour knelt, placed her arm around his neck and checked for breathing and a pulse. There was neither. There was a gash above his eye stained with dry blood. On the ground was a large pool of blood soaked into the soil. His body was cold and lifeless. At the later inquest into his death, it was determined that he had fallen, struck his head on a rock, been knocked unconscious and slowly bled to death.

Within minutes of discovering the body, all the searchers had gathered around in stunned, shocked silence, aside from whispers as people sought clarity and information. The whole scene suddenly changed when the missing boy's despairing parents ran over to the hushed crowd. People stood aside to let them through. Their pace slowed as they surveyed their son in the neighbour's arms and realised the obvious—he was gone. Their outpouring of inconsolable grief was beyond description as they knelt and took their son's lifeless body in their arms.

Sounds of grief filled the air. No one moved. In time, the parents' grief became private and silent. With a sobering and gut-wrenching sense of powerlessness, everyone realised that this death was preventable if they had found him sooner.

The farmer who had spoken earlier summed it up in a pertinent, almost inaudible, statement, 'If only we had joined our hands sooner!'

'If only we had joined our hands sooner!'

Reflection and discussion from Chapter Three: Selfless Unity (Part Two)

Personal Reflection:

1. *Adopt the attitude of a servant leader.* In reflecting on the principle of servant leadership, what wrong concepts of leadership have you had that need to change in order to conform to servant leadership? What behaviours or motivations do you need to adjust to display the traits of a servant leader?
2. *Pray for and with each other.* Take a few moments now to pray for each member of the team by name. What will you do to make the other team members a regular focus of your prayer?
3. *Support the team leader and his/her vision.* List the ways in which you support the team leader. Identify ways in which you will be more proactive in doing so.

Group discussion

Thinking about the content of this chapter, what one point do we need to prioritise to foster greater unity? What actions will we as a team employ to do so? Please pray for each other, then pray for your team leader.

SECTION III

CLEAR COMMUNICATION

CHAPTER 4
Clear Communication (Part One)

Clear communication is a third key principle in the harmonious relationships and productive function of a team. In this and the following chapter, I'll articulate a number of components for effective communication on a team.

1. SPEAK THE TRUTH IN LOVE (honest communication)

For communication on a team to be clear, it must be honest.

In the middle of a thought about Christians growing to maturity as a result of their unity and function in the body of Christ, Paul wrote that mature Christians won't be easily deceived by skilful liars, but '…*instead…will speak the truth in love…*' (Ephesians 4:15).

Paul did not just say, '*speak the truth*', otherwise this verse could be used as a spiritual disclaimer or immunity to be offensive, critical or judgmental. Importantly, Paul added the moderating words, '*in love*', so that it reads, '*speak the truth in love*'.

The qualifying words '*in love*' require us to ask questions such as: Is what I am about to say spoken from a motivation of love? Are these words for their good and to build them up? Am I speaking these words to resolve or to circumvent a potentially deeper issue or to divide? Will these words help this person to see deficiencies in their character, behaviour, relationships, marriage or life that need addressing?

In the first decade of the new millennium I was pastoring a fairly large church in Brisbane, Queensland. Our Eldership had regular prayer retreats when we would go away together to seek the Lord, pray about the church and do some strategic planning. One year, a senior leader from Britain, who I'd known and respected for some years, was in town. We invited him to come and observe how we operated as an Eldership and give us his reflections. Toward the end of our gathering, we specifically asked for his thoughts. After some affirmation, he insightfully asked, 'You guys obviously get along well together. You enjoy each other's company, but do you speak the truth to each other? Do you have the freedom to speak into each other's lives?' After a long, uncomfortable silence, we all conceded, 'No!'

Paul wrote of an occasion when he had to confront Peter, a fellow apostle, about what he deemed as hypocrisy in Peter's behaviour (Galatians 2:11-14). The setting was Antioch. When Peter first arrived, he ate with the Gentile Christians, but when some Jewish Christians arrived, he wouldn't eat with the Gentiles any longer. Paul wrote that Peter was '...*afraid of the criticism from these people who insisted on the necessity of circumcision*' to be truly saved (2:12). Peter's example resulted in other Jewish Christians, including Barnabas, also not eating with the Gentiles. Paul regarded this exclusion as '*hypocrisy*' (2:13) and inconsistent with '...*the truth of the gospel*' (2:14). So, Paul publicly confronted Peter for his double standard. If a man of Paul's spiritual calibre saw the necessity of reprimanding a person of Peter's apostolic stature and experience, then we, too, should speak the truth in love to one another.

Often in churches and Christian ministries, as long as everybody is *seen* to be getting on together, we don't say what needs to be said or talk about what needs to be talked about. In thinking about the team on which you serve, please reflect on the same two rhetorical questions posed to our eldership: Do you speak the truth to each other? Do you have the freedom to speak into each other's lives?

The following principles are practical ways in which we can speak the truth in love in a team context.

Don't be afraid to speak up if you genuinely are concerned about a decision the team is contemplating or a direction the team is considering

Nabal, whose name means 'fool', was a wealthy, land-owning descendant of Caleb. Incriminatingly, he was described as '…*crude and mean in all his dealings*' (1 Samuel 25:1-3). While David was a fugitive, Nabal's shepherds pastured their flocks in the locality where David and his men were hiding and were given protection by them (25:7-8,15-16). David subsequently heard that Nabal was shearing his sheep and he sent a delegation of ten young men to ask for provisions as an act of reciprocity. Nabal, however, sneered at the men and belittled David as an escaped slave leading a band of outlaws (25:10-12). When his men reported Nabal's response, David ordered them to get their swords. His intention was to kill Nabal and his household (25:12-13; 22).

Meantime, the shepherds reported to Nabal's '*sensible and beautiful*' wife, Abigail (1 Samuel 25:3), about the way David's men had been treated (25:14-17). Abigail wasted no time, but gathered provisions for David and his men, rode out to intercept them, and bowed low before David's feet (25:18-23). She spoke skilfully and reasoned with him by affirming his anointing as King. She pointed out his record in not doing anything wrong in his life to that date despite the injustices he had endured. She acknowledged that he had fought the Lord's battles, not his own (25:26-28). Abigail urged him not to pay attention to Nabal because he was a '…*wicked and ill-tempered man*', and pleaded with him not to blemish his record or conscience by 'needless bloodshed and vengeance' (25:25, 31).

Abigail's appeal affected David immediately. David praised the Lord for Abigail's 'good sense', and that she had kept him from '...murder and from carrying out vengeance' by his own hands. David received the provisions Abigail had brought him and sent her home in peace, assuring her that her husband would not be killed. The outcome of the story was that when Abigail told Nabal what David intended to do to him and his men, he had a stoke that paralysed him for ten days until his death (25:36-38).

Strictly speaking, Abigail wasn't one of David's team, but the principle in the story is that, because Abigail spoke up, David was prevented from pursuing a course of action that would have had disastrous consequences for his integrity and conscience. The application is not to be afraid to speak up if you are concerned about a decision or direction of the team on which you serve. But when you do so, please follow Abigail's example and speak with wisdom, tact and respect. Some people wrongly misinterpret speaking the truth as being tactless and blunt, but it is speaking lovingly, gently and appropriately, as Abigail did.

Some years ago, the Board of the church I was pastoring was given an investment opportunity that promised to yield a phenomenal return. One of the Board had done due diligence on the investment and everything checked out as legitimate. It would mean withdrawing some of the funds the church had invested securely in long term cash deposits with a bank and transferring them into an unsecured and risky venture. It was a significant sum of money. Everyone on the Board was in agreement, except for one man. He respectfully but firmly opposed this use of funds. His father had invested in a similar scheme many years before and lost everything. As a result, the family suffered greatly. His experience was very persuasive in shifting the Board's decision to reject the opportunity. I don't know whether that opportunity would have yielded the returns it promised but, based on other people's experience, I suspect we would have lost everything. This would have been disastrous on many levels. Losing so much money would have fatally eroded the credibility of the Board and my leadership. The point is that the dissenter was not afraid to voice his legitimate concerns.

> A healthy team welcomes a range of views, discusses them robustly, seeks to reach an acceptable position and moves forward.

On some teams there can sometimes be a culture of non-dissent. In other words, anyone with a contrary or opposing view is frowned upon and regarded as being out of step, not in alignment or not being in the spirit. A healthy team, though, welcomes a range of views, discusses them robustly, seeks to reach an acceptable position and moves forward. However, if/when you do raise a view or opinion contrary to the majority, please do so with the right attitude, and not simply to be recalcitrant or a 'devil's' advocate'.

Know what you want to say before you say it

On the Mount of Transfiguration, Jesus' appearance was transformed, his face *'shone like the sun'* (Matthew 17:2) and his *'clothes became dazzling white'* (Luke 9:29). Suddenly, Moses and Elijah *'...appeared and began talking with Jesus'* (Luke 9:30). Waking from a sleep, Peter saw this glorious sight and, as *'...Moses and Elijah were starting to leave, Peter, not even knowing what he was saying, blurted out, "Master, it's wonderful for us to be here! Let's make three shelters as memorials—one for you, one for Moses, and one for Elijah" '* (Luke 9:33, emphasis mine).

Peter didn't know what to say, but he spoke anyway. The lesson: don't just speak for the sake of speaking, but know what you want to say before you say it. If you have nothing meaningful to say, don't say anything. If you don't know what you're talking about, don't say anything. If you don't really know what's going on, don't say anything.

Everybody has an opinion, sometimes about things we know nothing about. This is particularly true in Western cultures. We form views, perceptions and opinions without any real firsthand experience, training or knowledge. If the topic is outside your knowledge base, don't say anything. Unless you're specifically asked to share your perspective, don't say anything.

Ensure you have sufficient relationship and rapport with another team member before bringing correction, offering advice or saying words that may be hard for them to hear

After news reached David that Absalom had been killed, he was overcome with emotion, burst into tears and retreated into an inner room above the city's gateway to mourn (2 Samuel 18:33). The triumphant troops, who had loyally fought for David, heard that he was weeping and grieving for his slain son. Consequently, '*…the joy of the day's victory was turned into deep sadness. They crept back into the town that day as though they were ashamed and deserted in battle*' (19:3-4). Despite having saved David and his family's lives, David's men felt demoralised and ashamed because of his despondency and anguish (19:5).

David didn't realise that, as a result, his leadership was on a knife's edge. At this critical moment, Joab, commander of David's forces, went to David and spoke very frankly about the affect his sorrow was having on the morale of the men. Joab bluntly and forthrightly directed David to '*…get out there and congratulate your troops,*' otherwise he gravely warned that '*…not a single one of them will remain here tonight,*' before adding that he would be '...*worse off than before*' (2 Samuel 19:7). David listened and took his seat at the town gate. Everyone gathered around him (19:8). Catastrophe was averted.

Another example is that of leprous Naaman, who left Elisha's home furious and affronted that Elisha did not show deference by seeing him personally, but sent his servant (2 Kings 5:10). To add to Naaman's sense of indignity, Elisha requested that he wash seven times in the Jordan River which, to Naaman, was a dirty stream compared to the rivers, Abana and Pharpar, in his home city of Damascus (5:12). Offended and insulted, Naaman headed home in a rage…and still leprous! (5:12)

At this point, some of Naaman's officers reasoned with him to obey Elisha's instructions (2 Kings 5:13). Naaman listened to them, softened his heart and dipped himself seven times in the Jordan River. The result was that Naaman's '...*skin became as healthy as the skin of a young child's, and he was healed*' (5:14).

Joab and Naaman's officers had sufficient standing and credibility with David and Naaman respectively to speak candidly with them about their attitude, actions and their possible consequences. Joab's seemingly stern words of warning prevented David from another rebellion and further upheaval. The persuasive words of Naaman's officers resulted in him being healed from a dreaded disease. The lesson here is for us to ensure that before we speak words that will be difficult for another team member to hear, we have a strong and solid rapport with them. Otherwise, our words may not be received.

Just as importantly, if we're on the receiving end of another person's counsel, correction or caution, we need to be humble and open enough to receive and process it. Many of the Proverbs encourage us to listen to such words because they will help us to become wise (12:15; 13:10; 19:20, 25), experience victory (11:14; 24:6) and gain understanding (15:31-33). Some Proverbs tells us to give attention and appropriate consideration to admonition (9:8; 12:1; 13:18; 15:31), but Proverbs 12:1 says that if we despise or disregard correction, we're unwise (cf. 13:13)! Words from a friend or someone close to us on the team may initially sting, but, in the long run, will do us good—if we learn from them (Proverbs 27:6; Psalm 141:5).

Don't be offended if no-one agrees with you or your point

Speaking the truth in love may sometimes mean that others will not agree with us. If they don't agree, if we don't get our own way, or if a decision is made that is contrary to our view, we have to ensure that we don't take offence or become bitter or antagonistic.

Sadly, however, it is my observation that people get offended so easily, often over minor issues or hurts. Some become moody or sullen, others withdraw, while still others develop resentment or bitterness. I have frequently seen offended people causing dissension and division. These subsequent responses and reactions display a lack of spiritual and emotional maturity.

My wife was originally from South Wales in the United Kingdom. We go there every few years to visit her extended family. Some of them from her father's side live in the historic, former Roman town of Bath. On one such visit, on a cold January day, we decided to do one of those tours on a double-decker 'jump on, jump off' red bus, which does a circuit of the major tourist sites. As we drove past one of Bath's picturesque parks, the audio narrative told us the following story.

The park was officially opened in 1830 by 11-year old Princess Victoria, who later became Queen Victoria, Britain's second-longest reigning monarch. It was to become the first park to carry her name. At the time, the press reported that Princess Victoria was dressed very 'dour'. This report didn't impress, and actually offended, the young royal. She made up her mind that she would never visit Bath again. She never did. But after the railway was established from London to Bristol, it passed through Bath. As the Queen's carriage approached Bath, she ordered her courtiers to close all the curtains on every window so that she couldn't see the people of Bath and the people of Bath couldn't see her. Until her death, Queen Victoria never saw or visited Bath again, all because she took offence at something that had been written about her.

> In a team context, just because someone disagrees with you doesn't mean they are rejecting you.

I urge you to guard your heart from offence. Maintain an attitude of forgiveness. Work things through and don't stew or simmer on things that were said or done. Keep your spirit uncluttered and unpolluted by the negative residue of bitterness or resentment.

In a team context, just because someone disagrees with you doesn't mean they are rejecting you. Just because others don't embrace your perspective doesn't mean your thoughts are invalid. Just because the team chooses to go a different direction than the direction you proposed doesn't mean what you suggested was wrong.

I'll conclude this sub-point with a few pointers on how to speak the truth in love. Say only what needs to be said–nothing more and nothing less. Say it because you mean it. Say it with the right motive. Say it with the right attitude. Say it with the right tone. Say it in love. Be as quick to listen as you are to speak.

2. UTILISE GOOD COMMUNICATION CHANNELS

For communication on a team to be clear, someone needs to be responsible for it and it must be conveyed by the most appropriate means.

The book of Hebrews opens with the statement, *'Long ago God spoke many times and in many ways to our ancestors through the prophets'*, but, the author continued, *'...now in these final days, he has spoken to us through his Son'* (1:1-2).

In the Old Testament, God primarily communicated to his people, especially the prophets, by various means, such as:

- Dreams and visions (Genesis 31:11-13; 37:3-11; Daniel 7-8);
- Audible and inward voice (Exodus 33:11; 19:19-24);
- Providential circumstances (Genesis 24:15; 1 Kings 22:29-37);
- Angelic visitation and message (1 Kings 19:1-8).

In the fullness of time, Jesus came as the Living Word, God in flesh, Emmanuel–God with us (John 1:1, 1:14). Jesus is the supreme way God has 'spoken' to us (Hebrews 1:2). Jesus was God's *messenger* as well as his *message* (and means) of salvation and redemption.

In the church age, God speaks to us by his Holy Spirit, who is his indwelling and empowering presence. In his final teaching to the disciples, Jesus spoke of how the Spirit will be given as his representative (advocate), who will be his continual voice reminding them of his words (John 14:26; 15:26; 16:13-15). John Stott notes that the Spirit *'...bears witness to Christ and to Scripture, and makes both living to the people of God today.'*[24]

> **The Lord used the most appropriate means and method to communicate his message to his people.**

Now, also, we have the Holy Scriptures, God's written Word. His Word is God-breathed, which is a way of saying that the Holy Spirit inspired men to record, explain and interpret God's words (speech), works (activity) and wonders (miracles). John Stott writes that the Bible '…is a *living word* to a *living people* from the *living God*, a contemporary message for the contemporary world.' God *has* spoken, God *still* speaks through what he has spoken and 'when God speaks he *acts*'.[25]

The Lord used the most appropriate means and method to communicate his message to his people. Similarly, if we are to communicate effectively as a team, we too must employ the most appropriate means and method suitable to our context and the content of our message.

There are many different ways for a team to communicate, such as: one-on-one (personally), phone, letter, email, text, social media, team meeting or public announcement.

To determine the most appropriate means, ask the following guiding questions:

- Who needs to know?
- Who needs to know what?
- In what order do they need to know?
- When do they need to know by?
- Who is the best person to communicate the information?
- What is the nature of the information? Is it sensitive or public?
- What is the appropriate mode of communication?
- What is the timeframe to communicate with the respective people or groups?
- Who will be responsible to ensure it is communicated?

A Bible example of this is seen in Acts 15 when the Jerusalem leaders of the early church had to decide on whether Gentile converts were required to be circumcised in order to be saved. After they had made the decision, it needed to be communicated. They had a methodical, organised plan to make the decision known. First, it was communicated to the Jerusalem church. In Acts 15:22 it states that the *'apostles and elders* together with *the whole church in Jerusalem decided to choose some of their own men and send them to Antioch with Paul and Barnabas'* (emphasis mine). This implies they communicated firstly with the congregation in Jerusalem. Secondly, according to the same verse (Acts 15:22), men were appointed to accompany Paul and Barnabas to represent the leadership and verbally report on the decision. Thirdly, they wrote a letter which contained the details of their decision for wider distribution (v. 23). Fourthly, they worked out where the letter would be read–*'To the Gentile believers in Antioch, Syria and Cilicia'* (v. 23).

It is vital to plan communication, delegate someone to take responsibility for it and have some mechanism to ensure the communication lines and channels are effective.

If the communication is of a sensitive nature, such as conflict-resolution or correction, never do so via email, social media or text. This should always be done personally, (wherever possible) face-to-face, and somewhere quiet so there will not be a disturbance or distraction. Written communication doesn't convey the heart, tone or facial expressions, and can easily be misinterpreted or misunderstood. To achieve resolution or reconciliation, it is always wise and best for it to be done one-on-one.

Communication is two-way. There may be someone responsible to communicate to the team, but there is also a responsibility on each team member to reciprocate, respond and understand what is being communicated. If you want something communicated to the leadership or other team members, communicate. If you don't understand something, ask. If you don't respond or acknowledge, how will the sender know their message been received?

Summing up, as God clearly communicates with us through whatever means he determines is best, so we must communicate with each other (on the team) through whatever channel is appropriate, depending on the nature of what needs to be said or conveyed.

3. DEVELOP LISTENING SKILLS (listen until we hear)

For communication on a team to be clear, it must be heard, understood (comprehended) and responded to.

Verbal communication involves more than just speaking; it also involves actively listening–the giving of one's undivided attention. This is not just listening with our ears (which is critical), but also with our heart, mind and spirit so that we really hear.

I go to sleep at night very quickly. One night, milliseconds before I descended into the tunnel of sleep, I thought I heard Fiona said, 'I love the dog.' I responded, 'Yes, she's a lovely dog.' Then her tone changed, as she reiterated, 'I didn't say, "I love the dog", I said, "I love my new job."' I wasn't listening properly, which, sadly, is not uncommon for me. It's something I'm endeavouring to work on.

Most of us in leadership and ministry have been taught or trained in how to speak, but very few of us have been taught or trained how to listen. Listening is critical in communication.

'Listening' is a theme in Scripture also. In the Hebrew language, the root word of both 'hear' and 'listen' is the word *sama* (pronounced shmah), a verb which occurs some 1050 times in the Old Testament. In most contexts the meaning extends beyond just the physical act of hearing to suggest processing and responding to what was said (cf. Exodus 15:26; Deuteronomy 6:4-5).[26] In fact, when translators translate *sama* they must decide whether, in the context, it means 'hear' or 'obey'. By way of example, when we speak to our children, we sometimes angrily ask, 'Did you hear me?' implying that they may have heard us but didn't obey us. This illustrates the Hebrew idea of *sama*. When we hear, we do so in the sense of hearing, processing and responding.

Jesus spoke of how his sheep must know his voice, listen for his voice and follow his voice (John 10:4-5). In the book of Revelation, Jesus asked that '...*anyone with ears to hear*...' in the seven churches of Asia Minor '...*must listen to the Spirit and understand what he is saying to the churches*' (Revelation 2:7, 11, 17, 29; 3:6,13, 22). Again, the emphasis is not just on audibly hearing words, but on active listening, then processing and responding to what has been said.

Applying this to the context of a team, the lesson is that we need to develop a capacity to concentrate and listen with the purpose of comprehension.

On average, people can speak at a rate of 125-175 words a minute (speed of speech), and our brains can process 400-800 words per minute (speed of thought) as words are being communicated to us.[27] The differential between the speed of speech and the speed of thought is one of the major reasons why many people have difficulty in listening. It is the root cause of distraction.[28]

As leaders, we need to be good listeners, so here are some ideas for how to develop the skills of being an empathetic listener. This list is adapted from Madelyn Burley-Allen's very helpful book, *Listening: The Forgotten Skill*.[29]

- Be attentive
- Be interested in the person you're speaking with
- Concentrate on what the person is saying
- Don't be in a hurry or give the impression that you're speaking to them to fill in time
- Seek to grasp what they are trying to say

- Mentally screen out distractions, like background activity and noise
- Maintain eye contact (or whatever is appropriate in your culture)
- Indicate you are listening by:
  - Brief expressions such as: 'I see', 'right', 'interesting' or 'I understand'
  - Non-verbal acknowledgement, such as: head nodding, facial and body expressions that are relaxed and open
  - Door openers such as: 'tell me more about it', 'would you like to talk about it?', 'let's discuss it', 'sounds as if you've got some ideas or feelings about this', or 'I'd be interested in what you have to say'
- Pay attention to what *isn't* being said–to nonverbal cues (such as their body language)[30]
- If listening for a long time, try to remember key words or phrases
- Keep an open mind; listen without judging or jumping to conclusions
- Where and when appropriate, respond to what has been shared with a view to engage in meaningful conversation

If the person starts sharing and baring their heart, here are some guiding principles for effective listening and responses:[31]

- Never minimise or trivialise what a person is feeling or facing
- Don't use stock phrases like, 'Oh, it's not that bad', 'You'll be better tomorrow', or 'It'll blow over. Don't be upset'
- Try to empathise; that is, try to feel what the speaker is feeling
- Share your own experiences to show understanding

- If you require clarity on something the person has said, wait for the person to pause
- Ensure you ask open-ended questions that require a thoughtful response, rather than closed questions that can be answered with just 'yes' or 'no'
- Endeavour to follow some ground rules for a conversation of this nature:
  - Don't interrupt
  - Don't take the subject off in another direction
  - Don't interrogate
  - Don't teach or preach
  - Do reflect back to the talker what you observe and how you believe the talker feels
- Guide and help them to see the solutions for themselves, rather than just tell them what to do.

> **'The most basic and powerful way to connect to another person is to listen.'**
>
> **Dr Rachel Naomi Remen**

One of the reasons I'm so strongly advocating for us to listen to each other is that it builds relationship, rapport and trust. It helps us to know and understand each other. Listening helps us to gain a full and accurate understanding of what the other person is saying or thinking. It's one of the tangible ways in which we sincerely show an interest and genuinely express what it means to be 'others-centred'.

Best-selling author, Dr Rachel Naomi Remen, wrote, 'The most basic and powerful way to connect to another person is to listen. Perhaps the most important thing we give each other is our attention.'[32]

Reflection and discussion from Chapter Four: Clear Communication (Part One)

Personal Reflection:
1. *Speak the truth in love*. Please reflect on the reasons why you sometimes withhold speaking the truth in love. From this reflection, what will you now change in your personal communication on the team?
2. *Utilise good communication channels*. Please write out ways in which you will communicate more effectively to each other and the team as a whole.
3. *Develop listening skills*. Out of the list of listening skills articulated in this point, please highlight three that you will cultivate.

Group discussion

In thinking about the point on speaking the truth in love, what can we do to create the right forums, culture and context so people can share openly and transparently with one another, the whole team and its leadership? Identify some of the communication problems we've had or do have on the team. Now, work out solutions.

CHAPTER 5
Clear Communication (Part Two)

In the previous chapter, we looked at the first three of six principles necessary for effective communication on the team. We looked at (1) speaking the truth in love, (2) utilising good communication channels and (3) developing listening skills. We'll now examine a further three principles.

4. ENCOURAGE EACH OTHER

For communication on a team to be clear, it needs to be in a positive atmosphere full of encouragement and affirmation.

The etymology of the English word 'encourage' is French, but derives from the Latin. The word is made up of two parts. The first part 'en' means 'in, into'. The second part 'courage' comes from Old French (*corage*) and means 'heart, innermost feelings, temper'. Over time, it evolved to mean 'valour' and the 'quality of mind which enables one to meet danger and trouble without fear'. As it adapted into English usage, it came to mean 'zeal, strength or bravery'.[33] Putting both parts together, the word 'encourage' came to mean 'to inspire with (or give) courage', 'to spur on',[34] 'to strengthen', or 'embolden' for a purpose.

In Scripture, the Hebrew and Greek words translated as 'encourage' (or derivatives) have similar meanings. Moses was instructed by the Lord to encourage his successor, Joshua, to lead the people to conquer and inherit the Promised Land

(Deuteronomy 1:38; cf. 3:28). After initially suffering heavy losses to the Benjaminites, the Israelites '...*encouraged each other and took their positions again at the same place they had fought the previous day*' (Judges 20:22). When annexed by Babylonian forces, King Hezekiah encouraged his military officers to remember that they had a greater power on their side (2 Chronicles 32:6-7).

According to Paul, some people in the body of Christ have the gift of encouragement, a divinely-endowed grace or capacity to comfort, strengthen and build others up in their faith (Romans 12:8).

Paul sent Tychicus to Ephesus and Colossae, and Timothy to Thessalonica, with a directive to encourage the churches (Ephesians 6:22; Colossians 4:8; 1 Thessalonians 3:2). When visiting the newly established churches in Lystra, Iconium and Pisidian Antioch, Paul and Barnabas '...*encouraged them to continue in their faith*' (Acts 14:22; cf. Acts 11:23; 16:40; 20:2).

In specific regard to leaders, Paul wrote to Timothy that his preaching should, among other things, encourage people (2 Timothy 4:2). Similarly, Paul urged Titus to '...*encourage the young men to live wisely*' (Titus 2:6) and encourage all his listeners to do all that he had taught (2:15), and ensure that elders be strong in the Gospel and the Scriptures so they '...*will be able to encourage others with wholesome teaching*' (Titus 1:9). Paul himself longed to visit the believers in Rome so that he could encourage their faith and be encouraged by theirs (Romans 1:12).

Armed with the assurance that Jesus is coming again and we shall be with him forever, Paul exhorted the Thessalonians to encourage each other (1 Thessalonians 4:17-18; cf. 5:11; Hebrews 10:25). Other places in the New Testament urge us to build one another up (Romans 14:19; 15:2; 1 Corinthians 14:26).

With these biblical examples as a backdrop, what can we do to encourage each other on the team?

> Create a culture of affirmation on the team by making encouragement a habit.

A first way to encourage others would be to intentionally and thoughtfully make it a habit of acknowledging and affirming someone on the team every time they do something that is meaningful, significant or impacting, whether large or small. A few simple words like, 'You did a great job', 'I really appreciate the little things you do that no-one knows about' or 'Thank you for being so faithful', could mean so much to someone. People who lack encouragement often feel undervalued, insignificant and unappreciated. We tend to be quick to criticise, but painfully slow to express encouragement. Let's reverse the order and create a culture of affirmation on the team by making encouragement a habit.

A second action is to encourage the discouraged. Most honest, self-aware leaders would concede that they have times of discouragement. The word 'discouraged' means to be deprived of courage, disheartened or lacking in confidence or enthusiasm. A way we can help others is to come along beside a discouraged person and do what we can to rebuild or restore their courage, confidence or heart. The following Bible story illustrates the point.

Prior to becoming king, David was once hiding from King Saul in a stronghold in the desert of Ziph. Saul's son, Jonathan, had come to him. There is a little phrase that we could almost glance over without really grasping the application. 1 Samuel 23:16 (NIV) reads, *'And Saul's son Jonathan went to David at Horesh and* helped him find strength in God' (emphasis mine). The suggestion here is that David was disheartened.

Understandably, life on the run was taking its toll on him emotionally, psychologically and spiritually. Jonathan had come expressly to encourage him. He did so by focusing David on the Lord his God.

Our text doesn't explicitly tell us *how* Jonathan helped him find strength, but the next verse gives a very big clue. *'Jonathan said, "Do not be afraid. My father Saul will not lay a hand on you. You will be king over Israel, and I will be second to you. Even my father Saul knows this"'* (1 Samuel 23:17). Jonathan helped him find strength in God by *affirming* the anointing, call and promise of God upon David's life. When people like Jonathan speak into *our* lives, our spirit is ignited and energised. We are enabled to keep serving as a leader with fresh resolve and resilience.

May each of us be like Jonathan and build others up. Let's speak words of 'life' into one another. May we affirm God's prophetic promises in other people's lives. There are probably disheartened people on the team just waiting for *us* to help them find strength in God.

Moses encouraged the despondent people at the impenetrable Red Sea not to be afraid of Pharaoh and his approaching army, but stand firm and see the deliverance the Lord would bring (Exodus 14:13). Isaiah encouraged the exiled people of Judah to remember the Lord their God, who promised he would hold them by the hand and provide divine help (Isaiah 41:13). On a number of occasions, Jesus had to encourage his fearful disciples not to be afraid (Matthew 14:27; 17:7).

I personally thrive on encouragement, especially after times when I feel I haven't preached or led too well. I have a minor speech impediment in the form of a mild stammer. On occasion, if I'm tired, jetlagged or nervous, I just can't get some words out. It can be deeply embarrassing. A few years ago, while speaking in a session at a denominational missions conference in the UK, I had one of my worst experiences ever. I just couldn't get the words out. I felt humiliated and highly embarrassed for my host. Next morning, he said to me, 'Great feedback from yesterday. One prominent pastor said it was the best presentation on strategic leadership he's ever heard.' That encouragement gave me fuel for the day ahead.

A third way we can encourage one another is with an *appropriate* gesture like a warm embrace, an arm around the shoulder, a thoughtful card or a personal gift. I speak to thousands of people each month and I rarely ever get any written feedback, so I am always touched when someone takes the time to write an email to express their appreciation for something I said.

There is an important distinction between encouragement and flattery. Flattery is when we say something for *our* benefit (to build ourselves up), whereas encouragement is when we say it for *their* benefit (to build them up). The motive of flattery is to ingratiate ourselves or promote our own interests, whereas the motive of encouragement is to embolden others and persuade them to fulfil their interests. Flattery makes us feel good about ourselves in the moment, whereas encouragement fills others with confidence and courage to pursue their longer-term goals and calling.

There's a pithy quote that reads, 'Gossip is saying behind their back what you would not say to their face. Flattery is saying to their face what you would not say behind their back.'

As a team, celebrate the victories, commend those who serve faithfully, affirm individual achievements, champion those who've accomplished something out of the ordinary, recognise those who've done something for the first time, acknowledge those who've stepped up to a new role, cheer on those who do something out of their comfort zone, and always look for opportunities to express appreciation. All of these actions help to foster an environment where encouragement is the normal vocabulary of the team, rather than the exception.

5. SPEAK WELL OF EACH OTHER AND TO EACH OTHER (and don't gossip)

For communication on a team to be clear, it must be positive both in public *and* in private.

The Apostle Paul gave clear instructions to the Ephesian church about the nature of their interpersonal dialogue: *'Don't use foul or abusive language. Let everything you say be good and helpful, so that your words will be an encouragement to those who hear them. Get rid of all bitterness, rage, anger, harsh words, and slander…'* (Ephesians 4:29,31; cf. Colossians 4:6).

We could paraphrase these verses by saying: speak well *of* each other and *to* each other from the heart. These verses have applicability to team communication because the way we speak to each other and about each other is critical to positive and productive communication on the team.

Paul mentioned that our *choice* of words needs to be positive when he wrote, *'Don't use foul or abusive language.'* In other words, we should choose our words carefully and slowly and not speak impulsively or without discernment as we did before we knew the Lord. In addition, he added that the *content* of our words should only be *'good and helpful'*. The stated reason he stipulates this is so that everyone who hears us may be encouraged by our words. He then addressed the *core* from which our words flow, which is our heart, mind and attitudes. To maintain good and helpful words that produce encouragement to

> **For communication on a team to be clear, it must be positive both in public and in private.**

those who hear us, we must ensure that we have thrown off the old sinful nature and former way of life and put on the new nature, allowing the Spirit to renew our thoughts and attitudes (Ephesians 4:21-24; Colossians 3:9-11; cf. James 1:19-21). This inner transformation and renewal is the only way by which we can be free of '...*bitterness, rage, anger, harsh words, and slander...*'

This does not mean that we'll never have a disagreement or tension with another person on the team. It does mean that when we inevitably do have friction or misunderstanding, we resolve them (as already discussed) quickly and biblically. A key to satisfactorily and maturely resolving any interpersonal issue is to maintain a right attitude toward the other party and always speak to them in a measured and respectful tone.

Importantly, speaking well of each other and to each other doesn't just relate to what we say in the public arena (to people's faces), but also in what we say in our private world (behind their backs). Both are essential to preserve integrity as a team.

The danger of gossip

An element of speaking well of each other and to each other is to avoid, at all costs, the destructive danger of gossip on the team. Gossip isn't fun or funny, but disruptive and corrosive to team communication.

Gossip has been defined as a conversation or report about unconfirmed facts, typically about people.[35] It is idle talk, innuendo or rumour about the personal and private affairs of others. American journalist and gossip columnist, Earl Wilson, quipped that 'gossip is when you hear something you like about someone you don't.'[36]

'A gossip' is a term we use to describe someone who habitually reveals personal, sensational or intimate facts about others.[37] In my view, to be called a gossip is one of the most unflattering and contemptible names one could ever be called.

Having a gossip on a team is potentially divisive and dangerous. A gossip is untrustworthy with sensitive information, cannot maintain confidentiality and is notoriously unreliable in covering the backs of their fellow team members. When someone is known as a gossip, it makes the other members of the team nervous and cautious. As someone once wisely cautioned: 'If you gossip *to* me, it's more likely you'll gossip *about* me.' People will then become very selective about the degree of personal disclosure they will bring to the team, primarily because gossip spreads like wildfire. Once spoken, it cannot be retrieved; it is like a broken egg or toothpaste squeezed from its tube.

Gossip creates fragmentation on the team because we tend to distance ourselves from people who spread malicious rumours or pass on unwelcome or unwarranted information. It's not because we're judgmental, but rather because we just don't trust them. Such barriers undermine the unity, harmony, trust and open communication of a team.

Instead, may each of us diligently abstain from gossip. Scripture condemns gossiping (Leviticus 19:16; Proverbs 11:13; 20:19). Let's heed the warnings of some wise people: 'What you don't see with your eyes, don't witness with your mouth.'[38] 'Do not repeat anything you will not sign your name to.'[39] If you don't know it as fact, then don't say anything. Even if it is true, what right have you got to spread it? The adage is true: If we've got nothing good to say about someone, then we should refrain from saying anything.

Another way to stamp it out on the team is by simply not listening to or entertaining it. If someone comes to you on the team and says, 'Have you heard about…?' please stop them before they utter another word. Tell them clearly that you don't want to hear about it. Lovingly but firmly challenge them not to pass on unsubstantiated rumours or unsupported insinuations about anyone. Also, reinforce the culture of the team that gossip has no place. In this way, you're stopping the spread of gossip and stopping the gossiper. As Proverbs 26:20 aptly says, *'Fire goes out without wood, and quarrels disappear when gossip stops.'*

6. CLARIFY TASKS AND RESPONSIBILITIES

For communication on a team to be clear, everyone must know *what* they're responsible to do and *who* they're responsible to.

One of the major communication problems on a team happens when team members don't understand the overall vision, how they fit into that vision, what's required of them or who they're accountable to.

Lessons from Jesus

Jesus had a clear and compelling sense of mission (Luke 4:18-19, 43; 19:10; Matthew 20:28; John 3:17; 10:10; cf. Isaiah 61:1-2; 1 Timothy 1:15). He knew what the Father had sent him to do. He called twelve young men to be his disciples to accompany him and be trained in mission (Mark 3:14-15). In time, Jesus sent the twelve out in pairs to practice what they had learned from his example and teaching (Luke 9:1-2). Before doing so, he gave them clear instructions (9:3-5), and, on their return, *'...they told Jesus everything they had done'* (9:10). Likewise, nearing the end of his ministry, Jesus chose seventy-two disciples, sending them in pairs to the towns and places he planned to visit on his next circuit (Luke 10:1). As he had done with the twelve, he gave them detailed instructions for specific situations (10:2-16). They, too, returned and joyfully reported that even evil spirits were subject to them (10:17).

There are many lessons we can learn from Jesus (as team leader), in the way he communicated with his disciples (his team) about their roles. The applications will be directed at both team leaders and team members respectively.

Team Leaders

A first application for team leaders is the importance of clearly knowing the team's mission (reason for existence) and vision (where you're heading). Jesus knew what he had been sent to do and what he wanted his team to do. Secondly, Jesus communicated and embodied his mission to the disciples. Thirdly, he empowered them with authority and sent them with specific instructions to do ministry for themselves. He listened to the reports from their ministry trips, answered their questions, brought clarity and correction when necessary, and in this way developed his team to continue his mission after his suffering, death, resurrection and ascension.

On one of my first field visits to Mozambique, I was being driven by a local team leader, who oversaw a team of rural church planters. While driving along between towns on a bumpy, orange-coloured, dirt track, I asked him what problems he was facing in being a team leader. He said, 'My team leaders don't do what I want them to do.' I asked, 'Do they know what you want them to do? Is it written down so they can refer to it?' He stared at me for a long time, even though he was still driving at high speed! It was a scary few seconds before he eventually said, 'I've never thought about doing that before.' I suggested he write a simple list of dot points outlining the responsibilities and expectations of his leaders. This was a revolutionary thought for him. A year or so later he told me how much his leaders had improved just by being given a one-page list of what he required them to do.

> For communication on a team to be clear, it must be positive both in public and in private.

Team leaders need to cast the vision clearly, regularly and creatively. Cast it in such a way that people understand it, embrace it and believe in it. Leadership consultant and author, Sam Chand, insightfully notes that understanding the vision '... isn't just about the *what* of ministry; it's also about the *why*. Leaders need to take time to communicate the "what" and "why" so people know the purpose and importance of what they're doing and are part of.'[40]

> **Team leaders need to cast the vision clearly, regularly and creatively. Cast it in such a way that people understand it, embrace it and believe in it.**

Articulate both verbally *and in writing* what you expect of the team and each person's individual role and responsibility. Make it short, simple and self-explanatory. Also explain who they are accountable to about what.

Team members

'Team communications are *everybody's* responsibility,' notes Chand.[41] Undoubtedly, it is the team leader's responsibility to *communicate* the vision, delegate tasks and responsibilities, but it is the responsibility of each team member to *understand* the vision, their tasks and responsibilities. Show initiative and seek clarity if you don't quite grasp the vision, your role in it, or the specific nature of what you're being asked to do.

If you don't know the team leader's vision, ask. If you don't know your responsibilities or expectations, ask. If you don't know why you've been asked to do a particular thing, ask.

Reflection and discussion from Chapter Five: Clear Communication (Part Two)

Personal Reflection:

1. *Encourage each other.* Thinking about your team, please identify at least one thing you can encourage each person about, then either call, text or email them to express your encouragement.
2. *Speak well of each other and to each other.* How will you apply this point to your week-by-week engagement with the other team members? What will you do to stamp out gossip on the team?
3. *Clarify tasks and responsibilities.* Do you feel you fully understand the vision of your church (or organisation)? Do you completely understand your role and responsibilities on the team? If the answer is 'no' to either one of these questions, what will you do to gain a greater understanding? Please write out your understanding of the vision and your role in fulfilling the vision.

Group discussion

What can we do as a team to create a greater culture of affirming and encouraging each other? What can we do to better understand, embrace, fulfil and communicate the vision?

SECTION IV

AUTHENTIC RELATIONSHIP

CHAPTER 6
Authentic Relationship (Part One)

A fourth relational principle of team is *authentic relationship*. This chapter will address the question of how can we develop genuine relationships with other team members.

1. BE REAL WITH ONE ANOTHER

If the relationships on the team are to be authentic, *we* (individually) must be authentic.

Authentic team relationships require every team member to be real, transparent, readable, honest and vulnerable. There must be no façades, masquerades, superficiality, showiness or charades in our life, otherwise the relationships could become shallow and artificial. The other members of our team must see and know the *real* us.

John 1:14 records that the '...*Word became flesh and made his dwelling among us.*' God's message (the Word) to humanity was Jesus' flesh-and-blood life. Jesus was God visible, God unveiled, God revealed and God on display. As such, people could see, hear and experience him. Jesus was completely authentic, sincere, knowable and engaging.

> **Like Jesus, our life must align with our message.**

Likewise, if we are to foster authentic relationships, we need to emulate Jesus by sincerely engaging with one another. Like Jesus, our life must align with our message.

Danger of inauthenticity

If, however, we lack integrity, display duplicity, guard parts of our life from scrutiny, or exhibit a pretence of spirituality but not the substance, we are in danger of being inauthentic. An inauthentic leader will lack credibility and trustworthiness. Consequently, their relationships on the team will always be deficient in intimacy and substance.

2. BE COMMITTED TO ONE ANOTHER

If the relationships on the team are to be authentic, we must be committed to one other. Elijah Maswanganyi and Kevin Conner wrote that '…the measure of success in the team will correspond to the measure of commitment from each person.'[42] In Scripture, we are required to be committed first and foremost to God, then to our families (Ephesians 5:22-6:4; Colossians 3:18-21), church (Hebrews 10:25), neighbours (Mark 12:31) and employers or employees (Ephesians 6:5-9; Colossians 3:22-4:1).

If we're truly committed to God, our lives will show evidence of this commitment, as follows:

- To love him with all our heart, soul, mind and strength
- To worship him in spirit and in truth
- To become like Jesus in character and conduct by the transforming work of the Spirit
- To obey him, his Word, commands and guidance
- To offer our bodies as a living sacrifice, wholly committed to him for his purpose
- To commune with him in prayer and listen to him through the Scriptures

- To live a godly life that gives glory to God
- To cultivate a happy, fulfilled marriage and teach our children about the Lord
- To be a witness by sharing our faith through personal evangelism and exemplary living

None of these commitments can be done half-heartedly, reluctantly, begrudgingly or out of some religious duty. Our commitment to God is a wholehearted and willing response to what he's done for us in Jesus Christ, how he has revealed himself in his Word and his unchanging character as the loving and living God.

Why should it be any different in our commitment to the other team members and the team's task? As we endeavour to give God our best, let's strive to give our best to the team and its work.

> **True commitment to the other members of a team would be characterised by dedication, devotion, loyalty, faithfulness and dependability one to the other.**

Commitment to the team should never be a mere obligation, duty or responsibility. On the contrary, true commitment to the other members of a team would be characterised by dedication, devotion, loyalty, faithfulness and dependability one to the other. It is an expression and extension of our commitment to God himself.

The language and the corresponding actions of commitment are summed up in the following statements. Commitment says:

> I am committed to you, I believe in you, I value you.

> I will support you, I will strengthen you, I will defend you.

I will encourage you, I will speak well of you, I will speak the truth to you.

I will stand with you, I will stand by you, I will stand up for you.

I will walk with you, I will laugh with you, I will cry with you.

I will be available for you, I will serve you, I will help you whenever I can.

I will pray for you, I will pray with you, I will trust for God's very best for you.

When Naomi urged Ruth to return to her people—the Moabites—as her sister-in-law had done, Ruth replied with words that capture the essence of commitment to another. She said, *'Wherever you go, I will go; wherever you live, I will live. Your people will be my people, and your God will be my God. Wherever you die, I will die, and there I will be buried. May the LORD punish me severely if I allow anything but death to separate us'* (Ruth 1:16-17). That's commitment.

A close friend of Fiona and mine recently lost her mother after a relatively short battle with cancer. It was a heart-wrenching time because our friend's mum was her sole parent and a remarkable woman. Our friend serves on the ministry team of a large church with several campuses. When news of the death broke, her team galvanised around her. Some brought meals to her home, others helped in the practical arrangements for the funeral service, others took over her responsibilities, but all of them were available to offer whatever support was necessary. I noticed how much the team were committed to each other. It spoke volumes of

> **Relationships don't just happen; they have to be built.**

the strength of the team and the level of commitment each one had for the others.

3. PROACTIVELY GET TO KNOW EACH OTHER

If the relationships on the team are to be authentic, we must purposefully and intentionally get to know the other members of the team.

Relationships don't just happen; they have to be built. There are some principles we can enact to form and foster relationships with the other members of the team.

Invest time into one another

A first action in getting to know each other is to invest time into team relationships. This happens as we prioritise and value relationships on the team.

Healthy teams make time to cultivate and improve their relationships and create opportunities to be together socially and not just on 'church' business. Some quick advice would be to go out together, have fun together, enjoy each other's company and always respect each other's time.

Many years ago, I heard of a study that was done analysing Jesus' use of time. The researcher noted that the gospels record only 53 individual days of Jesus' 3½-year ministry. In fact, he highlighted, John's gospel only records 20 distinct days. As he examined how Jesus allocated his time, he noted that Jesus spent more time with the twelve disciples than he did with everyone else combined. His conclusion was that Jesus' pattern was to invest more time with his team than he did with anybody else.

Despite the demands on Jesus' time, if he saw the value of prioritising his time to be with his team, how much more should we place a high value on allocating a high proportion of our time to team relationships.

Show an interest in one another

A second way to get to know each other is to genuinely show an interest in each other. Here are some ideas for how we can do so:

- Use their name when conversing with them; someone has well said that the most important word in any language is one's name
- Find out what interests they have
- Ask about their family and friends
- Give undivided attention when they are speaking; this demonstrates that we're genuinely interested in what they have to say and that we value them
- Develop the listening skills articulated earlier in this book

I have met a few extraordinary people over the years who exhibit great skills at showing an interest. Their body language, their choice of questions, their engagement with my responses, their undistracted focus as I spoke, their genuine interest in what I was saying, and their concentration and comprehension of what I was saying, made me feel that I was the most important person on the planet to them. We can all learn from people like this.

At other times, however, I've been at gatherings where the person I was speaking to was always looking around to see who was more important than I was to speak with. It always made me feel devalued. I determined never to be like that, but to speak with people as if they were the only person in the room.

Another quick tip for team members is to avoid being totally 'task'-oriented in our conversations, but ensure we always add a relational component.

The purpose of showing an interest is to seek to understand each other. As we really listen to what the other person is saying, and try to empathise or, in some cases, sympathise, we begin to gain an understanding into what makes that person tick and why they are like what they are like. In my experience, this is a great way to understand people.

Engage with one another
It almost goes without saying, but in order to establish relationships, we must engage with each other by talking, listening and being with them.

Keep a sense of humour
If we're happy, let's let our faces know. A smile shows that we are happy. Proverbs 15:13 says that a *'...glad heart makes a happy face'* and 17:22 states that a *'...cheerful heart is good medicine...'* Being happy does *us* good, but also does *others* good. A smile is contagious. A smile shows that we are pleased to see another team member and signals that we are welcoming and interested in them.

We sometimes under-estimate the influence of body language. Our body language can be like a second voice. It doesn't matter what we say—our body language underlines or undermines our words. Endeavour to relate warmly to people. Warmth is felt more than it's spoken.

In addition to smiling and being warm, have fun as a team. Know the appropriate time and place for humour. Be natural. Laugh at yourself. Laugh with others. Humour disarms and relaxes the atmosphere.

Tying this third point up, if we want the team to become more relational, we need to begin by becoming more relational ourselves by choosing to spend time with the other members of the team, showing an interest in them, seeking to understand them, engaging with them and having loads of fun.

Reflection and discussion from Chapter Six: Authentic Relationship (Part One)

Personal Reflection:

1. *Be real with one another.* Reflecting on your level of transparency with the other team members, to what degree would you say you're 'real' with them? Please write out specific ways in which you will be more authentic with the team.
2. *Be committed to one another.* Please list the ways in which you show commitment to the rest of the team. Now list what you will you do to show increased commitment to the other team members.
3. *Proactively get to know each other.* Thinking about this point, what one action from the three suggestions (i.e. showing an interest, engaging with and keeping a sense of humour) do you need to give attention? Please write out what you will do in practical response.

Group discussion

Candidly, what is the relational climate of our team? What can we practically do to become more relational? Thinking about this chapter, what are some of the barriers to authentic relationships? What will we do to dismantle them?

CHAPTER 7
Authentic Relationship (Part Two)

In Part One of our examination on how to develop authentic relationships, we covered the first three of six actions. We looked at the importance of (1) being real, (2) being committed and (3) proactively getting to know each other. In this chapter, we'll address a final three crucial principles to cultivate meaningful interaction.

4. DEVELOP TRUST IN ONE ANOTHER

If the relationships on the team are to be authentic, the team must trust each other.

For a ministry team to be cohesive, effective and productive, there needs to be a high degree of trust. Teams are made up of people who we trust, as we are trusted. Chand points out that 'mutual trust among team members is the glue that makes everything good possible.'[43]

Most definitions of trust describe it as a person's confidence or firm belief in someone else's honesty, integrity, transparency, ability or reliability. We need to have confidence our fellow team

> **For a ministry team to be cohesive, effective and productive, there needs to be a high degree of trust.**

members will do what they've committed to do and do it competently. We also need to have a belief that their character, behaviour and integrity is consistent with Christlikeness and Biblical principles, both in public and private. And we need to trust that they say what they mean and mean what they say.

Chand emphasizes that, 'Trust is important up, down, and across the whole organisational structure.'[44] This doesn't just mean trusting those who lead us, but also those with whom we serve on the team, and those we lead.

The concept of trust in Scripture

To really understand the type of trust we need to exhibit on a team, we need to fathom how Scripture describes 'trust'. In Hebrew, the words translated as 'trust' can mean 'to lean on' in the sense of 'depend' or 'rely', 'be confident', and 'to take refuge'. In Greek, the words translated as 'trust' can mean 'to hope' or 'to have confidence'.

The fundamental expression of trust is encapsulated by the phrase *'trust in the Lord'*. Trusting in God is the foundation of trusting others. There are many exhortations in Scripture to trust in the Lord (Psalm 37:3, 5; Isaiah 26:4; 50:10; John 14:1), but the one verse that captures the essence of fully putting our trust in God is Proverbs 3:5, which compels us to, *'Trust in the LORD with all [our] heart; do not depend on [our] own understanding.'*

At the heart of why we should trust God is God's trustworthiness. In other words, we can trust him because he is trustworthy. Because God is faultlessly dependable, utterly faithful, infinitely powerful and unchangingly holy, he can be fully trusted to do all he said he would do and be all he has revealed himself to be. Our response should simply be to trust in who he is as our God.

Scripture tells us that there are many facets of God's nature, character and works that we can put our trust in, such as his:

name (Proverbs 18:10); words (2 Samuel 7:28; Revelation 21:5-6); commands (Psalm 19:7; 119:86); unfailing and encompassing love (Psalm 32:10; 13:5; 52:8); and power (Ephesians 3:20).

In contrast, we are urged not to trust in anyone or anything as a substitute for trusting God. In this sense, the Bible tells us not to trust in: our own understanding (Proverbs 3:5; 28:26); other people (Psalm 118:8, 146:3; Jeremiah 17:5); idols (Psalm 135:18); our own resources or abilities (Isaiah 31:1); wealth (Psalm 52:7; Proverbs 11:28; Luke 12:13-21; 1 Timothy 6:17); human weapons against an enemy (1 Samuel 17:45; Psalm 20:7-8, 44:6-7; cf. Hosea 1:7); or our own human works to earn salvation (Romans 9:32, 10:3; Galatians 3:10).

> A trustworthy God requires that those who represent him in leadership also be trustworthy.

Succinctly, all of this means that because God is faithful, capable, dependable, truthful and responsible, he is unequivocally and unchangeably trustworthy. He will not and cannot fail us. Therefore, we are urged to have complete reliance on him. Trusting God assures us of hope and help.

Importance of being a trustworthy leader

A trustworthy God requires that those who represent him in leadership also be trustworthy. As defined by God's trustworthiness, this means that we must also be faithful (reliable), capable (competent at what we do), dependable (consistent), and, according to other Scriptures, keep confidences (Proverbs 11:13), be truthful (Exodus 18:21), honest in handling money (2 Kings 12:5; cf. Luke 16:10-12), integrous in business transactions (Deuteronomy 25:13-16; cf. Proverbs 11:1) and faithful to carry out a responsibility (Daniel 6:4; Luke

12:42). There must be no inconsistency, no duplicity, no half-heartedness, no negligence, no dishonesty, no untruthfulness and no unfaithfulness.

There are a number of examples in Scripture of trustworthy leaders: Hezekiah (2 Kings 18:5); Joseph (Genesis 39:6); Moses (Numbers 12:7); the supervisors entrusted with the money collected to rebuild the Temple (2 Kings 22:5-7; cf. 2 Chronicles 34:10-12); Daniel (6:4); and Paul (1 Thessalonians 2:4).

If, then, our teams are to be characterised and glued together by trust, we must take the responsibility to be a trustworthy leader. And, just as importantly, we must trust others.

How to be a trustworthy leader?

Here are some practical ideas for how to be a trustworthy leader:

- *Be authentic*. Chand suggests that trust grows in an environment that is HOT, which stands for Honest, Open and Transparent.[45] Being honest and real with one another builds trust.
- *Self-disclosure*. Acknowledging our personal faults, vulnerabilities or insecurities in a safe environment fosters trust.
- *Integrity*. Demonstrating impeccable integrity establishes trust.
- *Truthfulness*. Saying what we mean and meaning what we say reinforces trust.
- *Reliability*. Following through on our word and doing what we say galvanises trust.
- *Support others*. When other members of the team are going through a difficult or challenging season, do all you can to help, encourage and strengthen them. Be there for them. This cements trust.

- *Diligence*. Faithfully fulfilling our responsibilities strengthens trust.
- *Maintain healthy and positive attitudes*. Keeping a right attitude toward all those on the team preserves trust.
- *Exercise strict confidentiality*. We're only a trustworthy friend if we can be trusted with someone's confidence. Team members don't betray, undermine or backstab each other, but guard important information entrusted to them. This is critical for trust.
- *Take responsibility for wrong decisions or actions*. One of the most trust-building statements any leader can make is, 'I'm sorry. I was wrong.' Conversely, nothing destroys trust as quickly as a leader who blames others for their mistakes.

The ways trust is undermined on a team are the complete opposite of those mentioned in this list above. If we're: inauthentic, intentionally not sharing anything of a personal nature but portraying a façade, displaying duplicity, telling lies, exhibiting unreliability, demonstrating selfishness, not fulfilling our responsibilities, harbouring poisonous attitudes, not maintaining confidences, blaming others for our own failures, gossiping or betraying others, we will erode the relational integrity and harmony of the team.

How to trust others?

Here are some ideas on how to develop trust in others:

- Seek to make 'trust' your personal default setting for relationships on the team instead of scepticism or distrust. Adopt the attitude that says, 'I will trust you until you prove otherwise', rather than 'I don't trust you until you prove otherwise.' Most people mean well and endeavour to do their best, so form team relationships from a baseline of trust.

- Get to know the other team members. Trust normally grows when you get to know someone. Listen to them, seek to understand them, observe their behaviour and watch their interactions with others. I'm not suggesting you do this to look for shortcomings, but to look for the good.
- Don't be too idealistic, but realistic in your expectations of others. Don't expect from others what you don't do personally. Instead, embody everything you want the other person to be. Model the behaviour, attitudes and commitment you want from others on the team.
- If and when someone falls short of your expectations, don't immediately disqualify or distrust them. People make mistakes and have shortcomings. I have and I'm sure you have also. Instead, help them to learn from their mistakes. When a person learns from what they have done wrong, they become a bigger and better leader. Rather than distrust them, help them, coach them, equip them, invest in them and renew your trust in them.
- Don't pre-judge people. We often form an opinion of someone before we ever really get to know them. Pre-judging someone is how prejudices are formed. Instead, be objective, open-minded, open-hearted and don't draw assumptions too quickly, but guard your attitudes.
- Start small. If you've been hurt before and find it hard to trust people, start trusting people in the little things. Trusting someone's advice or trusting their ability to do a role is a way to begin rebuilding your trust levels. This could be a stepping stone to restoring trust in others. It may be some time before you would ever trust someone with a secret, but it is a proactive starting point. The danger is that if we don't start trusting people, we may keep people at a distance as a way to protect ourselves from possible further pain. This will produce barriers

on the team that aren't compatible with trust.

- If you've ever got question marks about someone's trustworthiness, please don't become standoffish or suspicious, but talk to your leader and, if appropriate, speak with the person themselves to clarify any issue.

> Trusting someone's advice or trusting their ability to do a role is a way to begin rebuilding your trust levels.

Give people the benefit of the doubt. If, after following these steps, you can't come to a point where you trust someone, please keep your attitude and relationship with that person civil for the sake of the team.

Breaching trust

Trust takes time to build and earn, but it can be broken in one of two ways. First, it can be instantly broken by a breach of someone's ethics, integrity, word or by their dereliction in fulfilling a vital responsibility. Or, secondly, it can be 'slowly eroded by countless relatively small but abrasive comments or actions' that undermine a person's credibility, character or competence.[46]

Danger of betrayal

One of the major things that shatters trust is betrayal. If you've been betrayed, you're not alone, but in good company. Here is a quick list of people who were betrayed in Scripture. Joseph's ten brothers schemed to kill him (Genesis 37:18-20). Delilah betrayed Samson's secret to the Philistines (Judges 16:18). Korah, Dathan, Abiram, and On, along with many community and council leaders, rebelled against Moses' leadership (Numbers 16:1-3). Gideon's son, Abimelech, connived with the people of Shechem and murdered his seventy brothers to become king (Judges 9:1-2,5-6). Absalom conspired against his father David (2 Samuel 15:1-4; 13-14). The jealous administrators and satraps (governors) of the Mede Empire colluded to find grounds for charges against Daniel (Daniel 6:4). Jesus warned that, due to persecution, some family members would betray them to the authorities (Matthew 10:21). As a sign of the end of the age, Jesus spoke of a great number of people turning away from the faith, betraying and hating each (Matthew 24:10). In fulfilment of a number of Old Testament prophecies predicting that the Messiah would be betrayed (Psalm 41:9, 55:12-14; Zechariah 13:6), Jesus was betrayed by Judas (Matthew 10:4, 26:16, 49-50; Luke 22:22, 48; John 13:21).

Sometimes a breach or betrayal of trust on a team causes irreversible and irreparable damage. As a result, many leaders can carry a lot of personal and unspoken pain, though most develop a capacity to conceal and disguise it. This can be detrimental to a leader on many levels unless it's exposed to God's healing power and processed.

That said, there's a big difference between painful memories and memories of pain. As a leader, I've been hurt more times than I can recall, but I only remember a few of them. I generally don't consciously relive or replay those incidents. It's unhealthy. But there are times when something triggers a memory. For a little while—less and less as time goes on—I remember the pain, but it no longer produces pain. It is a memory of pain, not a painful memory. If you're still carrying an unhealed, infected or crippling sense of pain, please ask the Lord to bring healing and, wherever possible, talk to someone mature to work it through.

The circumstance that brought me the most pain in leadership was the betrayal of someone whom I regarded as a close friend and ministry colleague. I can't even put into words the depth of feeling I experienced when I discovered what he'd done and said behind my back when I was in a vulnerable place.

The words 'gutted', 'shattered', or 'devastated' don't adequately describe my feelings. I felt that he should have defended, protected and supported me. Instead, he did the opposite. Of course, I'm not naïve enough to suggest that I was a perfect leader. Perhaps, if you heard his side of the story, there may have been some measure of justification in what he did. I don't know with any certainty. All I do know for certain is that some pretty underhanded things were done which caused me, my wife, family and many others a lot of grief.

Even though I forgave him, which was harder and took longer than I expected, and we've subsequently had a few amicable exchanges, I would find it very difficult to trust him again in a team context. I want the very best for him, I want his family and ministry to thrive and prosper, and I know he'd want the same for me, but I would be reticent to be on a team with him again.

I'm not saying that it's impossible to regain and rebuild trust; I am saying that it's infrequent and requires a great deal of vulnerability, difficult conversations and a lot of grace, prayer and time.

Trusting people after betrayal can take a long time. Because of pastoral roles I've fulfilled in the past, on many occasions I've sadly had to deal with couples where a partner has been unfaithful. Forgiveness normally comes at some point, but trust takes a long, long time to be restored, if at all. Just recently, I sat with a couple twelve months after the husband had confessed to unfaithfulness of a sordid nature. The couple were doing remarkably well. The grace the wife expressed and experienced was miraculous, a huge testament to her spirituality and maturity. The marriage, interpersonal communication and romance were now stronger than ever. I asked the wife how her trust levels were. Her facial expression changed to one of seriousness, and with a pensive look she answered, 'That will take time. Every time he goes away for work, I always wonder what he's up to. I'm not there yet.' Even though there had been forgiveness and the relationship was back on track, trust had not been fully restored. It takes a long time in a marriage and it's the same on teams.

5. DISPLAY LOYALTY TO ONE ANOTHER

If the relationships on the team are to be authentic, the team must be loyal to each other.

Strictly speaking, loyalty is the state of being loyal, and is regarded as allegiance, faithfulness or support for a person, group or cause. There can be loyalty to our favourite sporting team, or patriotic loyalty to our country, tribe, ethnicity or people. For others, loyalty is along political, partisan, ideological or religious lines.

> **When it comes to relationships, loyalty is not a feeling; it is a choice.**

In regard to teams, loyalty is a character quality we must all nurture to have sturdy and steady relationships. When it comes to relationships, loyalty is not a feeling; it is a choice. We choose to be loyal in good times and bad times, in tough times and great times, in times of growth and in times of decline, in times of peace and in times of attack, and in times of consistency and in times of change.

Of course, there will inevitably be differences among team members, but there must never be disloyalty, which manifests itself as a breach of confidentiality, betrayal of trust, breaking of solidarity or a disregard of friendship.

Loyalty has multidirectional expressions across the organisational structure: upward (to our leaders), across (to our fellow team members) and downward (to those we lead). We'll now explore all three.

Loyalty upward–toward our leaders

A first expression of loyalty on a team is to those who lead us (1 Thessalonians 5:12-13).

David set an incredible example of loyalty, despite it not being reciprocal. Saul, who burned with raging jealousy, tried to kill David on several occasions (1 Samuel 18:10-11; 19:9-10), and pursued him like a fugitive (1 Samuel 19:18-30:26). However, David's loyalty to Saul was uncommon and unmoved. David had opportunities to kill Saul, but he refused to do so, or permit his men to, even when an opportunity presented itself (1 Samuel 24:5-7). The stated reason why he was so loyal to Saul was that David recognised Saul as God's chosen and anointed ruler of Israel (24:6). Therefore, only God had the prerogative to remove Saul, not David. Loyalty toward our leaders comes out of recognising they have divinely-appointed authority.

Similarly, if we are to remain loyal to our leaders, despite how they may treat us, we must recognise their position of authority as God-given. We also acknowledge that it is solely God's prerogative to remove them, unless, of course, there is an issue of character or integrity requiring discipline.

Another example of loyalty is seen in the attitude in two of Noah's sons. After the flood waters receded, Noah, his family, and all the pairs of birds and animals aboard the Ark, left after it came to rest on Mt Ararat (Genesis 8:18). In time, *'Noah began to cultivate the ground, and he planted a vineyard'* (Genesis 9:20). He subsequently became drunk on some of his home brewed wine *'...and lay naked inside his tent'* (9:21). After discovering his father in this shameful state, Noah's youngest son, Ham, went and told his older brothers, Shem and Japheth (9:22). They, however, did not dishonour their father by looking for themselves, but held a robe *'...over their shoulders, and backed into the tent to cover their father. As they did this, they looked the other way so they would not see him naked'* (9:23).

After he sobered up from his stupor and learned what Ham had done in exposing his nakedness, Noah cursed the descendants of Ham's son, Canaan (9:24-25), but blessed Shem and Japheth (9:26-27).

What we learn from this account is that loyalty doesn't expose a fellow team member's weaknesses, vulnerabilities or indiscretions to public ridicule, as Ham did to his father. Instead, like Shem and Japheth, we do what we can to protect, support and encourage those who may have acted unwisely, immodestly or inappropriately.

I am in no way suggesting that we cover *up* someone's sin, especially a leader's, for that would be in violation of Scripture (1 Timothy 5:20) and, in some jurisdictions, a breach of the law. Covering *up* implies collusion and deception in helping someone (or an organisation) avoid or minimise the consequences of their actions. What I am suggesting is that, after someone's actions have been openly confessed and transparently dealt with, the team galvanise around the person concerned and cover them in solidarity, prayer and loving acceptance, until they are fully restored.

Loyalty horizontally—toward one another

A second expression of loyalty is not only to our leaders, but to one another on the team. To illustrate loyalty to one another, here are two biblical stories from two Josephs, who both remained loyal when there was justification to be disloyal.

A lesson in loyalty from Joseph—Jesus' earthly father

Matthew 1 records the circumstances of Jesus' birth. A lot of focus is placed on Mary, and rightly so, but she somewhat overshadows Joseph's righteous actions. Joseph was engaged to Mary, but '*…before the marriage took place, while she was still a virgin, she became pregnant through the power of the Holy Spirit*' (Matthew 1:18). At some point, Joseph was made aware of Mary's pregnancy, but did not, as yet, know it was a divine conception. Joseph would have been justified in dishonouring Mary, possibly exposing her to public scandal and ridicule, but Joseph *'...was a good* [righteous] *man and did not want to disgrace her publicly, so he decided to break the engagement quietly'* (1:19).

Even though Joseph, in all likelihood, must have felt betrayed, perhaps embarrassed, he didn't allow his own feelings to override how Mary must have been feeling. Two courses of action were open to him: Joseph could bring charges against Mary in court; or he could divorce her quietly in the presence of two witnesses.[47] But Joseph wanted to shield Mary from public humiliation and disgrace, so he considered a way that would honourably call off the marriage. He resolved to do this privately, so as not to draw unnecessary and potentially damaging attention to Mary.

While he was still contemplating this course of action, an angel of the Lord appeared to Joseph in a dream and instructed him not to be afraid to take Mary as his wife because *'...the child within her was conceived by the Holy Spirit'* and would be the promised Saviour prophesied by Isaiah (Matthew 1:20-23; cf. Isaiah 7:14). Joseph consequently obeyed the Lord and married Mary.

Joseph's selfless loyalty to Mary was exceptional. In applying this to our team, we note that before he understood what was really going on, Joseph stood by Mary when it would have been very easy to distance himself. We, too, must exercise loyalty to our team members even we don't understand them or their actions. Joseph put Mary's feelings and reputation above his own feelings and reputation. Loyalty means that we, too, must not just consider our own feelings, but be mindful of what other team members are going through and consider how they must be feeling. Even when he understood the gravity of what Mary was called to do, he too was willing to share in the divine call.

Not only had Mary been chosen to be the mother of Jesus, Joseph had equally been chosen to be the earthly father of Jesus. Loyalty also means that we must be willing to walk with others as God fulfils his purposes through them.

A lesson in loyalty from Joseph–the son of Jacob and Prime Minister of Egypt

Joseph's rejection by his jealous brothers, and his subsequent sale as a slave to Midianite traders, triggered a sequence of painful and unenviable circumstances in his life. Falsely accused by the seducing wife of Captain Potiphar, Joseph was innocently and wrongly imprisoned. Years later, he was negligently forgotten by Pharaoh's cup-bearer until two years after interpreting his dream of royal forgiveness and restoration. When he was appointed Prime Minister of Egypt, thirteen years had lapsed since his brothers' betrayal.

During the famine Joseph had predicted, Joseph's brothers had been sent to Egypt by Jacob to get grain for their diminished stocks and flocks. Unbeknownst to them, they actually appeared before Joseph to request grain. Some time elapsed before Joseph revealed his identity as their forgotten and forsaken brother. After Jacob's death, the brothers feared retribution for what they had done to Joseph. Joseph, however, displayed unusual kindness and loyalty to his brothers. Joseph understood that the providential hand of God had orchestrated his journey to, and elevation in, Egypt. He reassured them by saying, *'Don't be afraid of me. Am I God, that I can punish you? You intended to harm me, but God intended it all for good. He brought me to this position so I could save the lives of many people. No, don't be afraid. I will continue to take care of you and your children'* (Genesis 50:19-21).

From Prime Minister Joseph, we learn many things about loyalty. Though others may be disloyal to us, there is no defence for us being disloyal to them. As difficult as it is, we must treat them as God treats us: with undeserved forgiveness and a lot of grace. No matter what is done to us or said about us, we need to keep loyal for the sake of God's glory, God's providential will, the good of the team and maintaining a heart free from bitterness. We must also realise that some things we go through have a greater unfolding purpose we may not appreciate at the time.

Loyalty downward–toward those we lead

Loyalty isn't just displayed upward to those who lead us and those we lead with, but should also be displayed downward toward those we are leading. Jesus remained loyal to Peter, though knowing that Peter would soon disown him (Luke 22:31-32). Abraham rescued his nephew Lot and his family, after they had been captured by an invading army (Genesis 14:14-16), despite Lot selfishly choosing the fertile plains of the Jordan Valley, forcing Abraham to settle in the more difficult desert terrain to the west (Genesis 13:10-12). Barnabas stood by John Mark after Paul refused to have him accompany them because he had deserted them in Pamphylia (Acts 15:36-40).

> **Disloyalty devours relationships and disintegrates the effectiveness of the team and its purpose.**

Danger of disloyalty

One of the cancerous causes of a dysfunction on a team is disloyalty. Disloyalty has been described as unfaithfulness, betrayal, violating one's allegiance, treachery, or, as the Cambridge dictionary suggests, '…acting to hurt someone you are expected to support.'[48]

Disloyalty undermines team unity. Disloyalty devours relationships and disintegrates the effectiveness of the team and its purpose. Disloyalty toward those who lead us, or to our team itself, or to those we lead, is reprehensible and inexcusable.

6. KEEP A FORGIVING SPIRIT

If the relationships on the team are to be authentic, we must maintain an attitude of forgiveness and grace.

I've mentioned several times already that there can often be tensions and conflicts on even the best of teams. As I've recommended, when a relationship breaks down, sort it out biblically and quickly. One of the components of this is forgiveness.

When someone hurts us, we have a choice: We either choose to forgive or we have made a choice to become bitter. Forgiveness is *not* a feeling. It is a choice; in fact, it may be a *daily* choice for quite some time. If we're waiting for the *feeling* to forgive to come, it will never come. Forgiveness is a conscious and intentional act of our will. Feelings take time to heal *after* the choice to forgive has been made. Forgiveness is a hard choice to make. It takes courage and willpower. But it is a liberating choice.

Maybe you object to me asking you to forgive. Perhaps you're saying to me, 'If you knew what my ex-partner did to me…if you knew how my business associate ripped me off…if you knew how my Dad treated me…then you could *never* ask me to forgive. You just wouldn't understand.'

> We choose to forgive because we don't want to be tangled up on the inside with turmoil and resentment.

Forgiveness, however, is not minimising what happened to us, whether it was a loss of money, loss of innocence, loss of reputation or loss of family. Forgiveness is *not* saying that it didn't really matter, or that it didn't hurt. No, forgiveness says, 'It *was* wrong. *Very* wrong. It mattered. It hurt deeply. But I relinquish my right to hurt them for hurting me. I release the person, so I can be free. Therefore, I *forgive.*'

Often times, this means forgiving them even if they never say sorry. We forgive them for *our* sake, not theirs. We choose to forgive because we don't want to be tangled up on the inside with turmoil and resentment. We make the decision to forgive so that we don't become preoccupied and obsessed by the person. We resolve to forgive because we don't want what was done or said to eat us up any longer. And, as we'll soon see, we make up our mind to forgive because forgiving others pleases God.

Danger of unforgiveness

If we choose not to forgive, we've made a serious decision that has significant ramifications, not only for our lives, but for the team. Here are four potential hazards for a team if someone allows unforgiveness in their life.

Hazard #1: *Unforgiveness builds invisible barriers on the team*

When someone harbours an offence and refuses to forgive another team member, there will be an immediate chasm, unity will be disrupted, there is no longer oneness of heart and mind, Satan has a beachhead and the team's purpose is thwarted.

In the last church I pastored prior to joining World Outreach, we had a fairly large church auditorium. Every Sunday, I noticed that one family I was acquainted with sat on one side of the church, while another family I also knew quite well sat on the opposite side. I later found out that many years before I became pastor, the fathers of the respective families had had a falling out over a business transaction. Rather than sit together, sort it out and forgive, they immaturely decided to stay away from each other. The centre aisle of our church was like an invisible 'Berlin Wall' separating these two families. There is no place for this type of division on a team.

Hazard #2: *Unforgiveness produces bitterness*

Someone has quipped that bitterness is like drinking a bottle of poison and waiting for the *other* person to get sick. The *only* person we're hurting by not choosing to forgive is *our self*. Bitterness is toxic in that it poisons our thinking, emotions, and our relationships. In contrast, forgiveness is like a disinfectant and a decontaminant from the internal poisons produced by unforgiveness. Forgiveness enables us to be free from bitterness.

If we don't deal with bitterness, it can have disastrous effects. David's son Absalom carried bitterness for two years before it had devastating results. Absalom had a sister, Tamar, who was described as *'beautiful'* (2 Samuel 13:1). Absalom's half-brother, Ammon, fell in love with her and lusted after her. He became so obsessed with her that he became ill (13:2). Along with a crafty cousin, Ammon connived a devious plan to lure Tamar into his room (13:4-5). He then raped her (13:14). Ammon's love turned to a loathing hate, so he had his servant throw Tamar out of his room (13:17). The trauma, shame and disgrace were so severe that she *'...lived as a desolate woman in her brother Absalom's house'* (13:20).

When Absalom heard about what happened, he comforted Tamar, but never spoke a word to his rapist half-brother because he *'...hated Ammon deeply because of what he had done to his sister'* (13:22). He internalised his feelings for two years until he, too, conceived a sinister plan. He deceptively asked David for permission for all his male siblings, specifically naming Ammon, to attend a celebration. At the feast, Absalom had organised for some of his men to kill Ammon at his signal, which they did (13:28-29). When the murder was reported to

David, it was said that *'Absalom has been plotting this ever since Ammon raped his sister Tamar'* (13:32).

May we ensure that we don't have bitterness in our hearts because, whether we recognise it or not, it will corrosively affect our lives and will damage the team.

> **Forgiveness helps us to forget. Forgiveness empowers us to move on from the painful past.**

Hazard #3: *Unforgiveness preoccupies our memories*

If we do not choose to forgive, we will live like an incarcerated prisoner chained to their cell wall. We become prisoners to the past. Someone insightfully observed that unforgiveness produces 'past memories that are like ghosts haunting our present.'

Have you ever had a really bad photo taken of you? Imagine if you blew that picture up, framed it and hung it on the entry hall to your home for all to see. Wouldn't that be ludicrous? That is what some people do in their hearts if they don't forgive. The offence becomes like a framed picture in their heart. Consequently, the person remembers what they should forget and forgets what they should remember. Forgiveness helps us to forget. Forgiveness empowers us to move on from the painful past.

Hazard #4: *Unforgiveness affects our relationship with God*

This is the most serious aspect of unforgiveness, as Jesus taught us in the Sermon on the Mount. In what we call the 'Lord's Prayer' (Matthew 6:9-13), Jesus taught us to pray, *'...and forgive us our sins, as we have forgiven those who sin against us'* (Matthew 6:12). In some versions of Scripture, the word 'sin' is rendered 'debt'. Sin is likened to a 'debt' because it deserves to be punished.[49] Our sin is an unpayable debt to God. Jesus paid the debt through his sacrifice on the cross. He now offers full and free forgiveness *if* we come and turn from our sins and ask him to forgive us.

This short section of the Lord's prayer (Matthew 6:12) is the only portion on which Jesus elaborated: *'If you forgive those who sin against you, your heavenly father will forgive you. But if you do not forgive others, your Father will* not *forgive your sins'* (Matthew 6:14-15, emphasis mine). The implication is clear: *if* we forgive others, the Father will forgive us. However, he will *not* forgive us if we refuse to forgive others. Harbouring unforgiveness is very serious.

Why, then, should we forgive others? So that we will be forgiven of our sins. If we don't forgive, it means that we believe the person doesn't deserve it. It means that we think what was done to us outweighs what we have done against God. We need our eyes open to the enormous 'debt' we owe God.[50] Once we comprehend what he has done for us–the undeserving–we should also extend undeserving forgiveness toward others. This is the only way in which we can be fully and freely forgiven from our sins.

Similar, also, are Paul's words to the believers in Ephesus: *'Be kind and compassionate to one another, forgiving each other, just as in Christ God forgave you'* (Ephesians 4:32). Added to this are his words to the Colossian church: *'Bear with each other and forgive whatever grievances you may have against one another. Forgive as the Lord forgave you'* (3:13). Putting these verses together, the unmissable application is that those who have been freely forgiven by God must freely forgive others, even if it means forgiving the undeserving and unworthy, because this is what Jesus has done for us.

Reflection and discussion from Chapter Seven: Authentic Relationship (Part Two)

Personal Reflection:
1. *Develop trust in one another.* From the lists articulated in this point, what will you do to (a) be a more trustworthy leader and (b) be a more trusting leader? Be specific about the actions you will initiate.
2. *Display loyalty to one another.* Write out the ways in which you show loyalty to your team members. Then, list further attitudes and actions you need to develop to be a more loyal team member
3. *Keep a forgiving spirit.* In reflection, do you have any unforgiveness in your heart toward anyone on the team (or anyone in general)? If so, please deal with the unforgiveness before writing anything further. What will you do to ensure your heart remains free of unforgiveness in the future?

Group discussion

Thinking about the point on trust, what can we do to nurture a more trusting environment on the team? Identify the characteristics of a trusting team in terms of their behaviours, communication and relationships.

SECTION V

RESPECTFUL HONOUR

CHAPTER 8
Respectful Honour

A fifth and final relational principle of team is respectful honour. If our team is to interact in a biblical fashion, it must be characterised by a culture of honouring one another.

In conventional language, the English word 'honour' means 'high regard, respect, esteem.' We call a judge 'Your Honour' to respect their position in the community as arbiter and dispenser of justice. Honours are sometimes bestowed on people as a public recognition and acknowledgment of someone's act of bravery, outstanding community service or major scientific or medical discovery.

But, in Biblical language, the Hebrew and Greek words translated as *honour* have a different meaning. The Hebrew word comes from a root which means 'to be or become heavy, weighty.' When the word 'honour' was derived from it, it meant 'to honour' in the sense of 'to lend weight or esteem' or 'to acknowledge someone as weighty'. The word was always used in a social context, '...reflecting how people within a society evaluate someone,' so that if someone was closer to us, they would be 'weightier' in our estimation and esteem.[51] The Greek words in the New Testament translated as *honour* have a similar social meaning.

Scripture teaches that we are to honour a number of specific people:

- *Honour our parents* (Exodus 20:12; Ephesians 6:1-2; cf. Deuteronomy 5:16; Leviticus 19:3). The command to honour parents is the fifth commandment in the ten that Moses received on Mt Sinai. As Paul pointed out to the Ephesian church, it is the first command with an accompanying promise—namely that, if we honour our father and mother, '...*things will go well for you, and you will have a long life on the earth*' (Ephesians 6:3).

    Honouring our parents means that, as children, we must: recognise that their parental authority (with all the rights, responsibilities and accountability) comes from God; demonstrate respect toward them (Leviticus 19:3); obey them (Ephesians 6:1; Colossians 3:20); love them; and give proper weight, value and consideration to what they say (Proverbs 6:20).

- *Honour governing authorities*. Romans 13:7 explicitly tells us to '*give respect and honour to those who are in authority.*' This instruction to give honour to the governing (civil) authorities is the way by which we acknowledge that God has instituted government and civil leadership to regulate, order and administer our day-to-day lives.

    Because the authority of governments derive and operate under God's authority (Romans 13:1), Stott wrote that 'conscientious Christian citizens', will therefore 'submit to its authority' (except if what the State legislates contravenes the authority of God's Word),[52] respectfully 'honour its representatives' (Romans 13:7; 1 Peter 2:13-14, 17), 'pay its taxes' (Romans 13:6-7) and 'pray for its welfare' (Jeremiah 29:7; 1 Timothy 2:1-2).[53]

- *Honour everyone*. After writing about respecting governing authorities, Peter asked his readers to live '*honourable lives*' and to '*respect everyone*' (1 Peter 2:15, 17). 'Everyone' would encompass all those we come in contact with through our daily lives. In broadening its application, it would mean treating them with appropriate respect—irrespective of their rank, race, religion or socio-economic status, and valuing them as someone who has also been made in God's image, along with placing consideration on them.

> **Honouring others is an overflow of honouring God.**

- *Honour one another*. Romans 12:10 urges us to, *'Love each other with genuine affection, and take delight in honouring each other.'* This exhortation was addressed to a local church, but it is just as applicable to a team. May we take delight in honouring the other members of our team.

What does all this mean for our team? There are three things we need to practise if we are to 'honour' in a Biblical way.

1. HONOUR GOD

First and foremost, our compelling motivation in all we do as a team should be to honour God. This is the highest and greatest expression of honour. Honouring others is an overflow of honouring God.

There are compelling reasons why the Lord is worthy of honour. In the many references in Scripture to honouring God, we see that we should honour God because: everything belongs to him (1 Chronicles 29:11); he reigns over all (1 Chronicles 29:11); the whole earth is full of his glory (Isaiah 6:3); he is glorious and powerfully great (Psalm 29:1-2, 34:3); he is holy (Isaiah 6:3); he does marvellous things that were planned long ago (Isaiah 25:1); he is Creator of all things (Revelation 4:11); he sits on the eternal throne for ever and ever (Revelation 5:13); and, as the slain Lamb, Jesus is *worthy* of all honour (Revelation 5:12-13).

How do we honour God in practice? God's complaint to his people through Isaiah gives us some indirect insights: *'These people say they are mine. They honour me with their lips, but their hearts are far from me. And their worship of me is nothing more than man-made rules learned by rote'* (Isaiah 29:13). The people of Judah claimed to be God's people, but their hearts and words revealed otherwise. The people went through the motions of religious duty and said the right things, but their actual practice had degenerated into a mere tradition and lacked genuine love for God. Their hearts weren't in alignment with their profession of faith. Their so-called worship was not a genuine expression of reverential awe and admiration of God, but a repetitious liturgy of man-made rules.

Jesus applied this reference (Isaiah 29:13) to the Pharisees and teachers of the law (Matthew 15:8-9; Mark 7:6-7). He called them hypocrites for allowing traditions to be a substitute for their obedience to the commandments. Their hypocrisy revealed the true nature of their hearts. They had the knowledge of Scripture but distorted its application to suit their own traditions.

By way of application, if we claim to be God's people, our hearts will either substantiate or repudiate that assertion. Thus, a first way we truly honour God is by loving him with all our heart (Matthew 22:37-40; Mark 12:29-31; cf. Luke 10:25-29; Deuteronomy 6:5; 10:12). If we are to love him wholeheartedly, our lives must be *fully* devoted and consecrated to him and his service (Romans 12:1; 1 Corinthians 6:20; Proverbs 23:26). If our hearts and lives are fully his, we will obey his words and commands (John 14:15; 1 John 5:3; cf. 2:3-5; 3:22-24; Deuteronomy 26:16). In fact, obedience is a measure of our love for the Lord. If we love and obey him, we will worship him acceptably from our hearts with reverential awe as the eternal, unchanging, holy, transcendent, ever-present, all-powerful, Redeemer, King of Kings, Lord of Lords and Righteous Judge, whose Kingdom will know no end (Hebrews 12:28-30; cf. Exodus 3:5; Joshua 5:15; Psalm 33:8).

Jesus' life and ministry provide further insight into what it means to honour God. He said that his motive in all he said and did was to give glory to the Father (John 7:18; 14:13). He also spoke of how the completion of his redemptive mission would bring glory to God (John 17:4). In line with the Old Testament expression of honour, Jesus obeyed his Father (John 14:31; 15:10).

Putting all this together, to truly honour God we must love him with all our heart, consecrate our lives fully to him, live solely for him, obey him and his word, fulfil our God-given purpose, revere and worship him.

How do teams honour God?

Having explored how we individually honour God, what are ways in which a team can honour God?

- Ensure that the sole and prime *motivation* in everything the team does is to honour God. This encompasses the way we interact with one another, the way we discharge our responsibility, the way we treat our leaders, the way we live our lives in private and the way in which we engage with the broader community. All of these things must be done in a way that gives honour to God.
- Work at fulfilling the *purpose* of the team *wholeheartedly*. In the same way Jesus completed the mission given to him and brought glory to his Father, as we work with all our heart, with all the gifts God has given (1 Peter 4:10-11), toward the team's God-given purpose, we are bringing honour to God. Jesus spoke about how our good works and fruitfulness are ways in which the Father receives glory (Matthew 5:16; John 15:8).

- Love each other other sincerely. Jesus said that the greatest command was to love God with all our heart, soul, mind and strength. But, he added, that the second greatest command to *'love your neighbour as yourself'* was *'equally important'* (Mark 12:30-31). If we love God, we will love others. In the context of a team, this is expressed through our heartfelt and practical expressions of love for one another. As we do this, we honour God. Also, we demonstrate that we love him and his love is at work in our lives.

> **A biblically-functioning team, motivated to glorify God, working together harmoniously, toward a God-given purpose, will bring honour to God.**

- Endeavour that the *relationships* on the team are conducted in a way that brings honour to God. Essentially, this is applying biblical principles to how we form relationships on the team, how we speak to each other, how we get on with them, how we resolve conflicts, and how we selflessly give of ourselves to one another. According to Romans 15:5-6, if we *'...live in complete harmony with each other...*[we] *join together with one voice, giving praise and glory to God, the Father of our Lord Jesus Christ.'*

A biblically-functioning team, motivated to glorify God, working together harmoniously, toward a God-given purpose, will bring honour to God.

2. HONOUR OUR LEADERS

Secondly, honour should be expressed to our team leaders and spiritual oversight. The Lord Jesus, Paul and the author of Hebrews highlight the work of spiritual leaders as: giving spiritual guidance (1 Thessalonians 5:12); teaching the Word of God (1 Timothy 5:17; Hebrews 13:7); shepherding (providing oversight) of the people entrusted to them by the Holy Spirit (Acts 20:28; Hebrews 13:17); pastorally caring for people under their care (Acts 20:28); guarding them from dangers, such as false teachers and false doctrines (Acts 20:28-30); praying for them (2 Timothy 1:3; Luke 22:31-32); equipping them for spiritual service (Ephesians 4:12); and being an example of service, faith, godly character and mature conduct (John 13:15; 1 Corinthians 11:1; 1 Timothy 4:12; Hebrews 13:7).

We are explicitly told to *'…honour those who are [our] leaders in the Lord's work… Show them great respect and wholehearted love…'* (1 Thessalonians 5:12-13), *'… accept the authority of the elders'* (1 Peter 5:5), *'remember [our] leaders'* (Hebrews 13:7), *'obey [our] spiritual leaders, and do what they say* (Hebrews 13:17).

Drawing principles from these and other verses, we express honour to our leaders by the following attitudes and actions:

- Respect them and the spiritual role they fulfil under God (1 Thessalonians 5:12-13; 1 Timothy 5:17)
- Because of what they do as leaders, sincerely love them in word and action (1 Thessalonians 5:12-13)
- Remunerate them appropriately, especially those who teach and preach (1 Timothy 5:17)[54]
- Always refute negative or disparaging talk about them, and never be a sympathetic ear to critical people (1 Timothy 5:19; 1 Samuel 24:6-7)
- Be mindful and considerate of them (Hebrews 13:7)
- Do what they ask us to do with a good attitude (Hebrews 13:17)
- Respect and accept their authority (1 Peter 5:5)

- Thoroughly support them (1 Chronicles 12:18)
- Cover their back, defend them and stand with them (1 Samuel 14:7)
- Speak well of them both publicly and privately (Exodus 22:28; Numbers 12:8-9; 21:5-6; Acts 23:5; cf. Ecclesiastes 10:20)
- Share their burden by relieving some of the pressure of their responsibilities (Exodus 17:12; 2 Corinthians 7:5-7; 2 Timothy 4:11)
- Provide for their needs (Acts 28:10)
- Get on together (1 Thessalonians 5:13). The last sentence of this verse, which refers to honouring our leaders, is very pertinent because it reads, *'And live peacefully with each other.'* One of the ways we show honour and respect to our leaders is by getting on together (*living peacefully*)!

Honouring our leaders has both an inward and outward dimension. Inwardly, honour stems from a heart attitude of respect, esteem, value and right recognition of our leader's God-appointed position and responsibility. It comes from within.

Outwardly, our inward attitude of honour needs to be demonstrated through practical expressions, such as encouragement, support, meeting their needs or helping in hands-on ways.

A story from David's years on the run illustrates this point of expressing our honour. While the Philistine forces were camped in the valley of Rephaim, a group of three of David's elite fighting men visited him while he was hiding in one of his strongholds. *'David remarked longingly to his men,*

> **Honouring our leaders has both an inward and outward dimension.**

"Oh, how I would love some of that good water from the well by the gate in Bethlehem"' (2 Samuel 23:15). The Philistines had a detachment of soldiers occupying Bethlehem at the time. Nevertheless, *'...the Three broke through the Philistine lines, drew some water from the well by the gate of Bethlehem, and brought it back to David'* (v. 16). David refused to drink the water because he regarded it as precious as the blood of the men who had risked their lives to get it (v. 17). Instead, he poured it out as a liquid offering to the Lord (v. 16).

David's men showed great heroism when they brought refreshment to their leader. Their honour was not just an inward attitude, but an outward and visible expression of the value they placed on their leader.

I remember preaching on this story, found in 2 Samuel 23:13-17, at one of our leader's nights at the last church I pastored. I entitled the message 'bucket-bearers'. Next day, I went to drive home after a long day at the office. To my surprise, my car was washed and sitting beside it was an empty bucket. One of the young leaders had been touched by the message and did something meaningful to express his honour for me. I was really moved and humbled.

What can you do to be a bucket-bearer for your leader to bring refreshment as David's men did?

Danger of dishonouring leaders

I want to sound a note of warning about the danger of dishonouring leaders. Time after time, there will be tests of our attitude toward our leaders. Anyone who resents or resists being given instructions from their leader is a rebel at heart. Our attitude toward our leaders is the all-important thing. Maswanganyi and Conner wrote, 'One team member without a submissive spirit and attitude can disrupt the whole team. Strong will must not become self-will!'[55] Unaccountable people, such as Korah and the rebels he led against Moses (Numbers 16:1-

3, 13-14), are potentially disruptive and treacherous. Ungodly and undisciplined reactions to our leaders can do a lot of harm, both to the team itself and to our standing on the team. To avoid doing or saying anything dishonouring, let's ensure we keep ourselves accountable to our spiritual oversight, guard our attitudes toward them, muzzle our mouth from speaking negatively, and wholeheartedly persevere in serving the team and its cause.

3. HONOUR ONE ANOTHER

Along with honouring God and our spiritual leaders, if our team is to proactively foster a culture of honour, we also need to honour *one another* (Romans 12:10). Honouring people 'over' us is relatively easy, but honouring one another is sometimes not that easy. It demands initiative, thoughtfulness and mastery of our attitudes.

As with honouring our leaders, honouring one another has an inward and outward dimension. Inwardly, we honour the other members of the team by regarding them with appropriate respect, value and appreciation. This comes from recognising that they, like us, are made in God's image, purchased by Christ's blood, gifted by God, created to do good works, full of godly potential and equally valuable to the team (1 Corinthians 12:22-26; note vv. 24-25).

Flowing from an inward attitude, honouring one another also needs to be actively conveyed and demonstrated through word and deed. The following is a list of ideas for how we can show honour to the other members of the team. Many of these dot points have already been articulated throughout this book in other contexts, but are summarised to mention how we can exhibit honour to one another. We can do so by:

- Always being respectful in word, attitude and body language

- Not allowing any disagreements to simmer (Ephesians 4:26), but initiating reconciliation to resolve any interpersonal conflicts (Matthew 18:15)
- Writing thoughtful notes of appreciation and encouragement
- Giving gifts of thanks for someone's kindness or to celebrate a key milestone or achievement
- Commending them for doing something out of the ordinary or expected
- Encouraging one another
- Investing time in our relationship with each person
- Constantly being truthful and transparent
- Intentionally being supportive and committed
- Speaking well of them
- Trusting them
- Valuing their gifting and contribution to the team as of vital importance and equal value to our own
- Helping in practical ways, such as assisting them to shift or providing transport
- Putting their interests above our own

Referring again to Paul's metaphor of the many-membered body (1 Corinthians 12:12-31; Romans 12:3-8; Ephesians 4:1-16), Paul not only emphasised the diversity and distinction of each member (1 Corinthians 12:14), but also the necessity for all parts to value and care for each other. As God has arranged every organ, limb and muscle in its right place for the proper function of our physical bodies, so God has arranged every member of Christ's body in its right place for its effective and fruitful function. Paul stressed that the parts that '...*seem weakest and least important are actually the most necessary*' (12:22). Those that seem insignificant, weak or unnecessary are the ones Paul says we should '...*clothe with the greatest care...*

> There is diversity on every team, but there is also equality (not of responsibility, but of value and necessity).

carefully protect' and give '*extra honour*' (12:23-24).

In every church and on every team, there are those who are prominent and those who work behind the scenes, those that seem indispensable and those that seem replaceable, or, to employ Paul's words, those that are deemed honourable and those that are deemed less honourable. However, I repeat what I wrote earlier on unity: there is diversity on every team, but there is also equality (not of responsibility, but of value and necessity). There are no unnecessary members. Each one has a distinctive part to play.

By way of application, this means that we should not place a higher value on some team members as being more worthy of honour than others, but display and show equal value and honour to *all* members. Paul stressed that we should give extra care, protection and honour to those who seem or feel insignificant or don't have a prominent or public role. This is the way, wrote Paul, that promotes '*...harmony among the members, so that all the members care for each other. If one part suffers, all the parts suffer with it, and if one part is honoured, all the parts are glad*' (1 Corinthians 12:25-26). Therefore, let's do what we can to honour those members on the team that do not normally receive honour or recognition. In this way, we'll demonstrate what it is to truly honour each other.

Reflection and discussion from Chapter Eight: Respectful Honour

Personal Reflection:

1. *Honour God*. Write out all the things for which you are thankful to God. Then write out the reasons why, from your experience and knowledge of Scripture, God is worthy of honour, glory and worship. Take time to express your heartfelt honour and worship to God.
2. *Honour our leaders*. List the qualities and characteristics you appreciate about your spiritual leader(s). Please send a thoughtful email or card expressing your gratitude as an expression of honour. What will you do from now to continue expressing honour to your leader(s)?
3. *Honour one another*. From the list of suggestions of ways in which we honour other members of the team, please choose three that you can act on within the next few days. Write out the specific people and corresponding actions you have identified.

Group discussion

What can we change in terms of our motivations and actions to ensure we as a team are honouring God in all we do and are? What will we do to build a culture of honour on our team?

CONCLUSION

This book began by emphasising the important place of relationships for effective team work. In a Christian ministry context, for a team to fruitfully accomplish its purpose, it needs to be undergirded by visible, genuine and resilient relationships.

Because teams are a Biblical pattern and the most practical way to get a job done, we asked the question of how does a team work together relationally? We then journeyed our way through five relational principles of a team.

A first and pre-eminent principle of effective team ministry is 'tangible love'. The love we are called to express to our fellow team members has to be based on the model of Jesus' love for his disciples. Jesus instructed them to love each other '...*as I have loved you.*'

Jesus himself set the example for his team. He called them, and he calls us, to follow in his steps. He is not asking us to do any more than he himself has done. He has demonstrated and modelled the type of love he is looking for us to express. His love is the measure by which we measure our love. His love is the grounds on which we love one another. We are commanded to love one another because he first loved us. Jesus demonstrated how we are to love one another by his own example of identifying, serving and self-sacrificing.

When we love each other in the way Jesus commanded and envisaged, our team will display the evidence of a true loving community that will bear witness to the message of salvation in Jesus. Our loving team relationships will validate the truth of our gospel message.

'Selfless unity' was the second of the five relational principles. Based on Philippians 2:1-4, we explored six actions vital for oneness as a team. We examined the necessity of (1) working together in diversity, harmony, synergy, with the vocabulary and mentality of a team, fuelled by proactivity. Then, we highlighted the indispensable action of (2) agreeing together wholeheartedly by resolving any conflicts quickly and biblically. Delving deeper into the reference in Philippians, we covered the crucial thought of (3) being 'others centred', which means thinking less about ourselves and more about our fellow team members. Using the example of Jesus, we underlined the importance of (4) adopting the attitude of a servant leader and not allowing cultural views of leadership to distort a Kingdom view of leadership. Further, unity requires that we (5) pray for and with each other because, ultimately, being one is a work of the Holy Spirit. Finally, to avoid any division or disunity, we underscored (6) supporting our team leader and his/her vision unswervingly.

The third relational principle we examined was 'clear communication'. Once again, six practical ways to improve our team communication were proposed. Team communication must be (1) honest and spoken from a motivation of love. Added to this, the team needs also to (2) utilise good communication channels so that everyone knows what they're responsible to do, what's going on and who they relate to about what. This implies that we (3) develop listening skills, which means acquiring a greater capacity to concentrate, connect and comprehend what is being said to us. When (4) communication is delivered in an environment of encouragement and affirmation, the team builds itself up. Sustaining a positive atmosphere on the team requires that we (5) speak well of each other and to each other, both in our public and private conversations. In practical terms, if the team is to perform well, each team member needs to (6) clarify their tasks and responsibilities.

Drilling to the core, the fourth relational principle we identified and considered was 'authentic relationship'. Six actions were recommended to build authentic relationships. The first was the need to be (1) transparently real with one another, so there is no superficiality or concealment in our lives. A further way we can build relationships is to be (2) committed to one another. This requires that we are not passive in fostering relationships, but (3) proactive in getting to know each other. Importantly, team relationships need us to be (4) trusting and trustworthy, (5) show loyalty to one another, and, no matter what is said or done to us, we (6) maintain a forgiving spirt.

Finally, we saw that if we are to function relationally as a team, a fifth component is honour. We examined three expressions of honour. First, that the team must be motivated by honouring God in all that it is and does. Secondly, the team needs to express appropriate honour to its team leaders and spiritual oversight. Following on, thirdly, we noted the importance of showing impartial honour to each other on the team. All three are necessary to cultivate and continue a culture of honour.

I finish this book with some paraphrased prayers and exhortations from Scripture for you and your team. My heartfelt prayer would be that your team would be brought to complete unity (John 17:23) and be one even as our God is one (John 17:21). I ask that you '...*live in harmony with each other...*', that '...*there be no divisions...*', and that you'd '...*be of one mind, united in thought and purpose*' (1 Corinthians 1:10). I appeal to you not to be passive about this, but '*make every effort to keep yourselves united in the Spirit*' (Ephesians 4:3). Remember that we stand '...*together with one spirit and one purpose, fighting together for the faith, which is the Good News'* (Philippians 1:27).

Let's always keep in mind two vital, often overlooked, eternal goals of every team: to give glory to God and to faithfully share the gospel of Jesus Christ. This is *why* we must have great relationships on the team.

APPENDIX
Five Spheres of Christian Leadership

Diagram 1
Spheres of leadership

	Sphere	Focus of leadership	Scope of leadership
1	Self-leadership	Leading yourself	In and over your own life
2	Home leadership	Leading in the home	Fulfilling your family roles/responsibilities
3	Team membership	Leading *with* others	Functioning on a team with delegated responsibilities
4	Team leadership	Leading others	Leading a specific team or group
5	Organisational leadership	Leading leaders	Leading a church or organisation

As illustrated in the diagram above, I propose that there are five different spheres in which we can serve God in Christian leadership.

Summary of the five spheres of Christian leadership

Sphere 1: Self-leadership. This is the foundational sphere of leadership: leading ourselves. I define self-leadership, 'in a Christian context, as the intentional practice of disciplining, regulating and developing our lives and leadership toward God's purposes in us of maturity and mission.'[56] Before we can effectively lead others by our example and leadership skills, we must lead ourselves.

Sphere 2: Home-leadership. The second sphere of leadership is to fulfil our role and responsibilities within our family. It requires the loving and conscientious commitment to fulfil our biblical responsibilities as a wife (Ephesians 5:22-24), husband (Ephesians 5:25-33), child (Ephesians 6:1-3; 1 Timothy 5:4) or parent (1 Timothy 3:4-5; Ephesians 6:4). If, as Paul argues, a key criterion for church leadership, especially eldership, is to have one's family life in order, then we must give attention to our home responsibilities. Stott comments that learning to lead in our family is a 'training-ground' for leading in God's family (the church).[57]

Sphere 3: Team membership. This third sphere of leadership is when we become part of a team or group with specific responsibilities. It involves working and serving *with* people. We may not have the responsibility of a team leader, but we have a responsibility to discharge a duty as one member of a team.

This book is framed within this third sphere.

Sphere 4: Team leadership. A fourth sphere of leadership is when we assume responsibility to lead a team. Team leadership requires a different set of skills, qualities and competencies to team membership, but being part of a team is a preparatory step in developing leadership experience. People serving as a team leader recognise a grace, gift and call of God upon their lives to lead (Romans 12:8). In response, they develop their God-given gifts, leadership skills and abilities to do so effectively.

Sphere 5: Leading leaders. The fifth sphere is when we become an organisational leader that leads leaders. Once again, a more enlarged skillset and mindset are necessary. These abilities and proficiencies must be acquired or developed to provide the calibre and competency of leadership required for leadership at this level.

Diagram 2
Concentric circles of the five spheres of Christian leadership

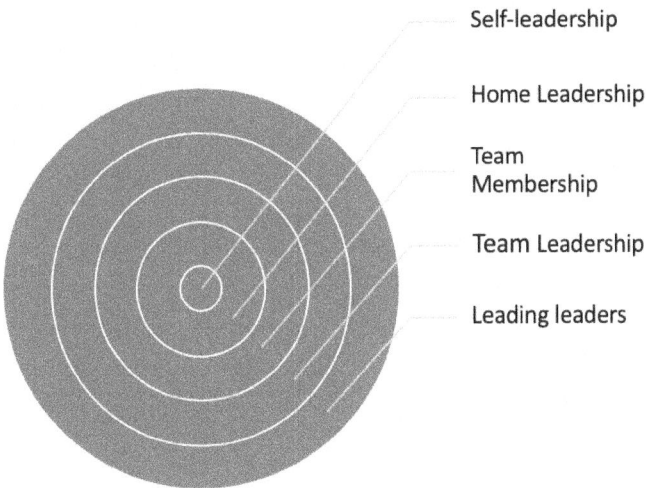

- Self-leadership
- Home Leadership
- Team Membership
- Team Leadership
- Leading leaders

While not everyone is called, gifted or skilled to lead a team or a church/organisation (spheres 4 and 5), almost all leaders will serve *with* others on a team (sphere 3). So, the first three inner spheres in the diagram above—self, home and team membership—are foundational to *all* Christian leaders. As I stressed in my book *Inside Out*, in a Christian ministry context, we do not lead from the 'top-down (hierarchically)', but from the 'inside-out (incarnationally)'.[58] Therefore, we need to lead ourselves (self-leadership), conscientiously take a lead in our home responsibilities (home leadership), and ensure our relationships on the team are healthy (team membership), before we are biblically qualified to lead others and lead leaders. The spheres of leadership, which reflect our scope of influence, should spiral out from the core through the concentric circles. Ideally, as we grow and mature in each sphere, we become prepared to transition into the next.

BIBLIOGRAPHY

Beasley-Murray, George R., *Word Biblical Commentary: John*, Nashville, TN: Thomas Nelson, 1999.

Bromiley, Geoffrey W., *Theological Dictionary of the New Testament: Abridged in One Volume* (Edited by Gerhard Kittel and Gerhard Friedrich), Grand Rapids, MI: Eerdmands, 2003.

Burley-Allen, *Listening: The Forgotten Skill*, New York, NY: Wiley, 1995.

Chand, Sam, *Cracking Your Church's Culture Code*, San Francisco, CA: Jossey-Bass, 2011.

Flanagan, Neil and Finger, Jarvis, *Just About Everything a Manager Needs to Know*, Brisbane, Queensland: Plum Press, 1998.

Giles, Kevin, *Team Ministry – Theological Foundations*, Paper presented to students, Ridley College, Melbourne, Victoria, 1998.

Green, Michael, *The Message of Matthew* (The Bible Speaks Today, series editor: John Stott), Leicester, Great Britain: IVP, 2000.

Haggai, John, *Lead On,* Waco, TX: Word, 1987.

Hills, Bruce, *Inside Out: A Biblical and Practical Guide to Self-Leadership*, Brisbane, Queensland: CHI, 2017.

Jackman, David, *The Message of John's Letters* (The Bible Speaks Today, series editor: John R.W. Stott), Leicester, Great Britain: IVP, 1996.

Maswanganyi, Elijah and Conner, Kevin, *Biblical Principles of Leadership: Two are Better Than One*, Tzaneen, South Africa: Christ is the Answer Global Ministries, 1991.

Newman, Barclay M. and Stine, Philip C., *A Handbook on The Gospel of Matthew*, (USB Handbook Series), New York, NY: United Bible Societies, 1988.

Richards, Lawrence, *Expository Dictionary of Bible Words*, Grand Rapids, MI: Zondervan, 1985.

Schaeffer, Francis A., *The Mark of the Christian* (Second Edition), Downers Grove, IL: IVP, 2006.

Stott, John, *The Message of Romans* (The Bible Speaks Today), Leicester, Great Britain: IVP, 1996.

Stott, John, *The Message of the Sermon on the Mount* (The Bible Speaks Today), Leicester, Great Britain: IVP, 1996.

Stott, John, *The Message of 1 Timothy and Titus*, Leicester, Great Britain: IVP, 1996.

Stott, John, *I Believe in Preaching*, London, Great Britain: Hodder and Stoughton, 1982.

Warren, Rick, *The Purpose Driven Life: What on Earth Am I Here For?* Grand Rapids, MI: Zondervan, 2002.

Endnotes

1. Although the word 'Trinity' is not used in Scripture, there is ample evidence of God's oneness (Deuteronomy 4:35-39, 6:4; Exodus 20:3; Mark 12:29; Galatians 3:20; Ephesians 4:6) *and* plurality or triunity (Matthew 3:16-17, 28:19; John 14:16-17; 1 Corinthians 12:4-6). The term 'Trinity' sums up the Christian doctrine of God: three persons of one substance or essence.
2. Peter and John ministered together at the healing of the crippled man at the temple gate called Beautiful (Acts 3:1-11). Philip (the evangelist), along with Peter and John (apostles), worked together to establish the gospel in Samaria (Acts 8:14-17). Peter and six other 'brothers' journeyed to the gentile home of Cornelius (Acts 10:23). Judas and Silas (prophets) joined Paul and Barnabas (apostles) at the Jerusalem Council to debate the issue of whether circumcision was necessary for gentile converts (Acts 15:22).
3. Adapted from Kevin Giles, *Team Ministry - Theological Foundations*, pp. 2-3. Giles lists the following examples. Barnabas and John Mark accompanied him on his first missionary journey (Acts 13:1-6). Silas joined him on his second journey (Acts 15:40), where they were joined by Timothy en route (Acts 16:3). Priscilla, Aquila, Aristarchus, Luke and Erastus were also members of the team on this third journey (Acts 18:23-21:17). Demas, Epaphras, Tychicus and Trophimus are all mentioned working with him while he was in Rome. Erastus, Titus, Tychicus, Timothy and John Mark are all mentioned in the pastoral epistles as ministering with him in the last part of his work.
4. Some technical facts adapted from https://www.nationalgeographic.com/animals/birds/e/emperor-penguin/ and https://en.wikipedia.org/wiki/Emperor_penguin
5. ibid.
6. David Jackman, *The Message of John's Letters*, 101.
7. ibid, 131.
8. ibid, 101.
9. George R. Beasley-Murray, *Word Biblical Commentary: John*, 248.

10. Francis A. Schaeffer, *The Mark of the Christian*, 29.
11. The context is church leaders agreeing together to impose discipline on a person who refuses to reconcile after offending (sinning against) a brother. Because of the leader's agreement, and the spirit of Christ among them, what they decide on earth will be ratified in heaven.
12. Geoffrey W. Bromiley, *Theological Dictionary of the New Testament*, 1292.
13. https://www.merriam-webster.com/dictionary/unity.
14. https://www.vocabulary.com/dictionary/unity.
15. Neil Flanagan and Jarvis Finger, *Just About Everything a Manager Needs to Know*, 233.
16. ibid, 232.
17. ibid, 233.
18. Hills, *Inside Out*, 226-228.
19. Examples of people who humbled themselves are: the exiles under Ezra (Ezra 8:21); King Ahab (1 Kings 21:29); King Josiah (2 Kings 22:19); King Rehoboam (2 Chronicles 12:6-7, 12); some of the people from Asher, Manasseh and Zebulun (2 Chronicles 30:11); and people seeking the Kingdom of Heaven (Matthew 18:4).
20. Examples of people humbled by the Lord are: the Exodus generation in the wilderness (Deuteronomy 8:2, 16); Nebuchadnezzar (Daniel 5:20); the people of Judah under King Ahaz (2 Chronicles 28:19); the proud (2 Samuel 22:28; Job 40:12; Daniel 4:37); David's descendants because of Solomon's sin (1 Kings 11:39); those who exalt themselves (Matthew 23:12; Luke 14:11, 18:14); and the synagogue leader accusing Jesus of breaking the Sabbath (Luke 13:17).
21. Rick Warren, *Purpose Driven Life*, 148.
22. John Haggai, *Lead On*, 59.
23. Michael Green, *The Message of Matthew*, 215-216.
24. John Stott, *I Believe in Preaching*, 15.
25. ibid, 100, 103.
26. Lawrence Richards, *Expository Dictionary of Bible Words*, 331.
27. https://www.skillsyouneed.com/ips/listening-skills.
28. https://listenlikealawyer.com/speed-of-speech-speed-of-thought.
29. Madelyn Burley-Allen, *Listening: The Forgotten Skill*, 127-128.

30. https://www.forbes.com/sites/womensmedia/10-steps-to-effective-listening.
31. Some points in this list are adapted or quoted from Burley-Allen, *Listening: The Forgotten Skill*, 127–128.
32. https://www.skillsyouneed.com/ips/listening-skills.
33. https://www.etymonline.com/word/encourage.
34. https://www.merriam-webster.com/dictionary/encourage.
35. https://en.oxforddictionaries.com/definition/gossip.
36. http://www.wiseoldsayings.com/gossip-quotes/.
37. https://www.merriam-webster.com/dictionary/gossip.
38. Jewish Proverb retrieved from http://www.wiseoldsayings.com/gossip-quotes/.
39. Unknown origin.
40. Chand, *Cracking Your Church's Culture*, 48.
41. ibid, 48.
42. Elijah Maswanganyi and Conner Kevin, *Biblical Principles of Leadership: Two are Better Than One*, 59.
43. Chand, *Cracking Your Church's Culture Code*, 51.
44. ibid, 51.
45. ibid, 51–52.
46. ibid, 53.
47. Barclay M. Newman and Philip C. Stine, *A Handbook on The Gospel of Matthew*, 22.
48. https://dictionary.cambridge.org/dictionary/english/disloyal.
49. John Stott, *The Message of the Sermon on the Mount*, 149.
50. ibid, 149.
51. Lawrence Richards, *Expository Dictionary of Bible Words*, 342.
52. Some examples of this in Scripture are: the midwives who disobeyed Pharaoh's order to kill the male Hebrew newborns (Exodus 1:17); Shadrach, Meshach and Abednego, who refused to obey Nebuchadnezzar's idolatrous law to bow to the image of gold (Daniel 3:12; 16–18); likewise Daniel, who refused to submit to the law instituted by King Darius that no-one could pray to any god or man for thirty days except him as King (Daniel 6:10); and Peter and John who refused to obey the Sanhedrin's demand not to preach in the name of Jesus (Acts 4:18–20).
53. John Stott, *The Message of Romans*, 347.

54. The NLT renders 1 Timothy 5:17 as: *'Elders who do their work well should be respected and well paid'*, but other versions have *'worthy of double honour'* (NIV, NASB).
55. Maswanganyi and Conner, *Biblical Principles of Leadership*, 60.
56. Bruce Hills, *Inside Out: A Biblical and Practical Guide to Self-Leadership*, 7.
57. John Stott, *The Message of 1 Timothy and Titus*, 98.
58. Hills, *Inside Out*, 6.

About the Author

Pastor Bruce Hills (B Min, MA Theo)

Bruce has been in Christian ministry since 1984 and brings a wealth of experience and wisdom. He is known and respected around Australia for his prophetic and insightful preaching. One well-known Christian leader in Asia described him as having the 'precision of a teacher, but the fire of a prophet'. Bruce frequently travels to many nations speaking at seminars and conferences. For nine years (2000-2009) Bruce pastored one of Australia's largest Pentecostal churches. He now serves as International Director for World Outreach International, a mission agency with a vision for unreached people groups.

Bruce has authored three other books, *Praying with Power – How to Engage in a Deeper Level of Personal Prayer by Praying the Scriptures; Fearproof – How to Overcome the Paralyzing Power of Fear – exploring the 'do not fear' statements of the Old Testament*; and *Inside Out – A Biblical and Practical Guide to Self-leadership*. Bruce has been married to Fiona since 1983 and has three grown children and one granddaughter. They live in Melbourne, Australia.

Visit www.world-outreach.com for more information on the author.

www.ingramcontent.com/pod-product-compliance
Lightning Source LLC
Chambersburg PA
CBHW061650040426
42446CB00010B/1671

WHAT OTHERS ARE SAYING ABOUT THIS BOOK ...

I have known Bruce Hills for over 40 years since we were friends as teenagers. Bruce has always had a passion for God and for the extension of God's Kingdom. This book reflects that passion. Bruce writes from both his own personal experiences as a leader in many different scenarios and also from the depth of his knowledge of the Word of God. From these frameworks he presents both Biblical principles of leadership and practical guidelines to become an effective and fruitful leadership team. Many emerging and current leaders and team members will greatly benefit from this book.

Dr Daryl Potts
Lecturer on Practical Theology, Program Director of Associate Ministry Degree and Bachelor of Ministry Degree Alphacrucis College, Sydney, Australia

I have known Pastor Bruce for many years. I have seen in him a shepherd's heart, and how he deeply cares about the growth and training of pastors around the world. What characterizes him is that he lives what he teaches. Pastor Bruce has visited Egypt many times to train pastors and leaders. We have translated his previous books, *Praying With Power, Fearproof* and *Inside Out*, into Arabic. The Lord has used these books to train hundreds of other leaders.

I'm looking forward to translate this book, and praying that it too would be a blessing to many others.

Dr Nathan Bassaly
Ministry Leader, Cairo, Egypt

Teams are intrinsic to God's master plan for His church. In this book, Bruce presents key non-negotiable principles essential to team health and resulting effectiveness. His insights are not only gleaned from Scripture, but also borne out of experience.

Together: Five Enduring Principles for Effective Teamwork will be an invaluable resource to use in understanding the dynamics of both leading and serving on a team founded on clear Biblical principles. Indeed, it's a great induction manual! I would particularly recommend this book as a must read for those serving in higher levels of leadership.

Graham Shand
Lead Pastor – Aspire Church
Founder & Director – Mentoring Matters for Pastors & Leaders
Melbourne, Australia